G000122256

# RECIPES FROM THE FRONT LINE

**First published October 2000**
by Forces & Corporate Publishing Ltd,
Hamblin House, Hamblin Court, 92-94 High Street,
Rushden, Northamptonshire NN10 0PQ, England
Telephone: 01933 419994
Email:fcp@netmatters.co.uk
Website: www.forcespublishing.co.uk
Managing Editor: Katie Mordue
Designer: Kerry Mountford

**ISBN 0-9529597-5-5**

# PROJECT TEAM

| | |
|---|---|
| Caz Dyer | Editor |
| Sue Adamson | Publicity and Editorial |
| Sally Crawford | Art and Design |
| Vicky Dalton | Secretary and Editorial |
| Caroline Dean | Distribution |
| Sue Dugmore | Advisor |
| Jacqui Hine | Funding, Book Production, Editorial and Accounts |
| Debbie Howard | Launch |
| Flt Lt B James | RAF Marham Liaison Officer |
| Michelle King | Editorial |
| Flt Lt R Moir | Deputy RAF Marham Liaison Officer |
| Sqn Ldr P O'Neill | RAF Advisor |
| Wg Cdr P C Osborn | Chairman of Meetings |
| Sara Osborn | Launch |
| Jo Postlethwaite | Launch and Funding |
| Katie Wigston | Funding, Book Production, Editorial and Charities |

# Contents

# INTRODUCTION AND EDITOR'S ACKNOWLEDGEMENTS

This book originated from an idea by Sue Dugmore, the Station Commander's wife at RAF Marham. The idea soon gathered momentum with the project team's desire to raise as much money as possible for our two charities: Make-A-Wish Foundation and The RAF Benevolent Fund. The project team chased celebrities, hassled agents and raised funds. The end result is a book which is packed with delicious recipes and interesting anecdotes from some of your favourite celebrities and the world of the Royal Air Force.

It only remains to thank and acknowledge the individuals who have made this book possible.

# RAF Acknowledgements

AVM P O Sturley MBE BSc FRAeS
Gp Capt I L Dugmore ADC BSc
Gp Capt S J Hillier DFC MA BA
Gp Capt C M Nickols MA
Gp Capt N E Threapleton BSc
Wg Cdr S E Armitage-Maddox MBE
Wg Cdr M J Henshaw (Ret'd)
Sqn Ldr E H Bulpett (Ret'd)
Sqn Ldr A Fox-Edwards BSocSc
Sqn Ldr J Harrison MHCIMA
Sqn Ldr J M Paige
Sqn Ldr K W Willox
Flt Lt A S Burns BSc
Flt Lt J P Hughes BSc
Flt Lt C McKee BA
Flt Lt F Swanson
Plt Off J M Hawthornthwaite
Plt Off D Munslow
Sgt L Spencer
Cpl G Mount

# Civilian Acknowledgements

Mrs Katie Mordue (Forces and Corporate Publishing Ltd)
Miss Kerry Mountford (Forces and Corporate Publishing Ltd)
Mr Dave Brown (Forces and Corporate Publishing Ltd)
Mrs Helena Anderson (artwork contributor)
Dr Lisa Chamberlain-James
Mr Ken Delve (chapter four)
Mrs Tina Fox-Edwards
Mrs Fay Fradgley
Mrs Kath Hawker
Mr David Higham (RAF Benevolent Fund Enterprises)
Mr Andrew Higgie
Ms Fiona Lindsay (Limelight Management Limited)
Mrs Jo Maunder
Ms Liz Merrick (Make-A-Wish Foundation)
Mrs Janette Nickols
Mr Hans Onderwater
Mr David Reger
Mrs Micheline Sturley
Mrs Nicky Ward
Mrs Katherine Williams

The project team would also like to thank the many other people who supported and helped to bring this book to print.

## Make-A-Wish Foundation®UK

*Granting Wishes For Children Suffering*
*From Life Threatening Illnesses*

**Charity Registration No: 295672**

**Charity Registration No: 210848**

# FOREWORD BY KATE ADIE

An army marches on its stomach. And the RAF flies on - well, bacon butties, as far as I can remember at thirty thousand feet. One of the good things to associate with an aircraft approaching a landing-strip in the middle of nowhere, is that if it has Royal Air Force painted on the fuselage, there is likely to be some sort of food inside.

Ever since an early trip in a plane loaded with complicated equipment and lots of electronics, I've been aware that there's no point in stooging around in the clouds on an empty stomach; and the RAF is up to the challenge.

Those on the ground, and at sea, are also attached to provisions as well as munitions; the most urgent question asked in the Middle East desert during the Gulf War was not 'where is the Artillery/the fuel store/communications centre?' but 'where is the field kitchen?'

What more appropriate then, than Recipes from the Front Line? An idea which came from Sue Dugmore, the Station Commander's wife at RAF Marham, backed by a team of RAF wives, and all in a good cause - two in fact: The RAF Benevolent Fund, and the Make-a-Wish-Foundation. The Benevolent Fund delivers care and practical help to a large number of people, making them part of the extended family of the RAF - just one big family, as it describes itself. And Make-a-Wish waves a wand to create real magic for children with life-threatening illnesses: at any one time, there may be 140 wishes in the process of being granted. So enjoy the recipes - and the tales - and the food from the front line.

# CHAPTER ONE
# RECIPES FROM FRONT LINE
# CELEBRITY CHEFS

# Ainsley Harriott's
## Munchie Mustard
## Chicken Escalopes

**SERVES 4**

4 large chicken breast fillets

4 tablespoons olive oil

2-3 tablespoons Dijon mustard

1 garlic clove, crushed

1 loaf of ciabatta

1 teaspoon lemon juice

snipped fresh chives to garnish

salt and freshly

ground black pepper

For the salad:

50g (2oz) baby spinach leaves

1 bunch of watercress,

large stalks removed

½ small radicchio lettuce

4 tablespoons mayonnaise

1 tablespoon Dijon mustard

*'The idea of this dish is to cover a chunk of toasted ciabatta with baby leaf salad (buy a bag of ready prepared leaves if you wish), add a piece of the grilled chicken escalope and finish it off with a good dollop of mustard mayonnaise. Delicious! Happy munching.'*

Place the chicken breasts one at a time between 2 large sheets of clingfilm and beat out gently with a rolling pin until they are about 5 mm (¼ in) thick and have almost doubled in size. Mix 3 tablespoons of the oil with the mustard and the crushed garlic. Brush some of this mixture over both sides of the chicken, season with salt and pepper and set to one side.

For the salad, place the prepared leaves into a bowl and lightly toss together. Mix the mayonnaise with the mustard and set aside with the salad.

Cut the ciabatta in half lengthways as if you were going to make a sandwich and then across into 4 chunky pieces. Place cut-side down on the barbecue and leave for a couple of minutes until lightly toasted. Remove and set aside. Barbecue the chicken over medium-hot coals for about 3 minutes on each side until golden on the outside but still juicy in the centre.

Whisk the rest of the olive oil, lemon juice and some salt and pepper into the remaining mustard mixture. Add to the salad leaves and toss together lightly. Place a piece of ciabatta on to each plate and spread with a little mustard mayonnaise. Sprinkle over a few leaves, then put the chicken on top, followed by more leaves. Add another dollop of the mustard mayonnaise and sprinkle with a few snipped chives. Serve the awaiting munchers.

# ANTONY WORRALL THOMPSON'S
## PROSCIUTTO WRAPPED RICOTTA
## STUFFED CHICKEN BREAST

Mix all the cheese, Parma ham, basil and seasonings together. Divide the mixture into two.

Lay the chicken breast out flat, and with a small sharp knife make a slit at one end of the breast, using your fingers push down to the other end of the breast. You must work gently and carefully so as not to break the skin.

Take one batch of stuffing and push it through the pocket in the breast. Repeat with the other breast.

Rub the skin with olive oil, sea salt and ground black pepper. Wrap each breast in two slices of Parma ham. Heat a griddle pan and brown the chicken on both sides.

Place on a baking tray and bake in a pre-heated oven to 180°C/350°F/ Gas mark 4 for 20-25 minutes until cooked.

Serve with mixed salad leaves or rocket.

### SERVES 2

85g (3oz) ricotta

85g (3oz) buffalo mozzarella

30g (1¹/₂oz) freshly grated Parmesan cheese

25g (1oz) finely chopped Parma ham

basil leaves, ripped

pinch of freshly grated nutmeg

sea salt and ground black pepper

2 x large organic chicken breasts, skin and bone removed

olive oil

4 slices of Parma ham

mixed salad leaves/rocket to serve

# JAMIE OLIVER'S
## TRAY-BAKED PORK CHOPS WITH HERBY POTATOES, PARSNIPS, PEARS AND MINTED BREAD SAUCE

**SERVES 4**

8 pork chops
or 4 double pork chops
1 x rosemary, garlic and lemon
marinade (see opposite)
3 parsnips
3 smooth-skinned pears
680g/1¹/2lb
potatoes, scrubbed
salt and freshly
ground black pepper
1 x minted bread
sauce recipe (see opposite)

*'When I make this dish I ask my butcher to slice me a two-rib pork chop. I then ask him to lose one of the ribs and a little of the fat and to bat the meat out slightly, leaving me with a huge pork chop that looks fantastic.'*

Rub and massage the pork chops with the rosemary marinade and, ideally, leave for 1-6 hours for maximum flavour. Preheat the oven to 220°C/425°F/gas 7. Wash the parsnips and pears and slice into quarters lengthwise, removing the cores from the pears, then cut the potatoes into 0.5cm/¹/4 inch thick pieces. Dry them with kitchen paper, then put them into an appropriately sized roasting tray with the parsnips, pears, pork chops and the marinade. Toss over to lightly coat everything then season and roast in the oven for 45 minutes to an hour, depending on the size of the chops.

While the chops and veg are cooking, make the minted bread sauce. It's great smeared all over the pork.

# Jamie Oliver's
## Rosemary, garlic and lemon marinade

Mix everything together and massage on to your chosen meat.

Leave the meat in the marinade until you're ready to cook it.

# Jamie Oliver's
## Minted bread sauce

Finely chop 3 parts mint to 1 part bread and stir in some olive oil until the mix has 'loosened'. Then balance the flavours by carefully seasoning, adding the mustard and splashing in some vinegar to taste. The flavour improves with time.

**SERVES 4**

3 handfuls of fresh mint

1 handful of chopped bread

extra virgin olive oil

salt and freshly ground black pepper

2 teaspoons mustard

red wine vinegar

# PAUL GAYLER'S
## GRILLED MACKEREL WITH SWEET AND SOUR RHUBARB

4 tablespoons olive oil

200g (7oz) canned tomatoes, drained and finely chopped

325g (12oz) fresh rhubarb, peeled and cut into small chunks

3 tablespoons brown sugar

2 tablespoons balsamic vinegar

salt and freshly ground pepper

pinch of ground cinnamon

pinch of ground ginger

1 tablespoon chopped fresh coriander

4 fresh mackerel, about 400g (14oz) each

Mackerel is classically served with a gooseberry sauce; the point is that it needs a sharp flavour to offset the oiliness of the fish, such as this tangy rhubarb sauce.

Heat half the olive oil in a wide saucepan, add the tomatoes and simmer over a low heat until they become thick and pulpy. Add the rhubarb, brown sugar and vinegar and bring to the boil, then reduce the heat and cook gently for 8-10 minutes or until the sauce is thick. Season to taste with salt, pepper, cinnamon and ginger; you may need to add a little more sugar if the rhubarb is very acidic. Add the fresh coriander to the sauce and keep warm.

Clean the mackerel, remove the fillets and cut three small incisions into the flesh on both sides. Season and brush them with the remaining olive oil. Place under a hot grill and cook for 5-6 minutes on each side or until golden and crisp.

Serve the grilled mackerel with the rhubarb sauce, accompanied by some sautéed aubergine slices.

# Patrick Anthony's
## Cheerful chilli chicken

Slice the chicken in half lengthways then finely across the grain. Process to a paste the green chillies, garlic, fish sauce and sugar.

Heat the oil in a wok or sauté pan and stir-fry the mixture for about 1 minute then add the chicken and continue to fry until almost cooked through. Add the yellow pepper and red chilli and when the chicken is fully done mix through the basil leaves and serve with freshly washed and seasoned bean sprouts.

### Serves 2

350g (13oz) boneless, skinned
free range chicken breast
2 fresh green chillies
2 garlic cloves, peeled
1 tablespoon Thai fish sauce
(nam pla)
2 teaspoons soft brown sugar
2 tablespoons groundnut oil
1 yellow pepper, deseeded and
diced
1 red chilli finely diced
10-15 fresh basil leaves
fresh bean sprouts to accompany

# Tessa Bramley's
## WOK COOKED TUNA LOIN WITH A GINGER AND ORANGE MARINADE, NOODLES AND PICKLED GINGER

2 steaks of tuna loin - each about 125g/4oz - skinned and pin boned

4 tablespoons light soy sauce

zest and juice of 1 orange

squeeze of lemon juice

2 pieces dried root ginger - bruised with a rolling pin

2 cloves garlic - skins left on and bruised with a rolling pin

2 teaspoons cumin seeds - dry-fried and crushed

1 tablespoon brown sugar

3 tablespoons nut oil (preferably almond)

1 small glass Amontillado sherry

125g/4oz cooked egg noodles

a little pickled ginger

several stems of fresh chives

Start the fish in the morning if possible - a few hours in the marinade greatly improves its flavour.

Make marinade: Pour soy, orange juice, lemon juice and oil in a non reactive dish. Add zest, sugar, ginger, garlic and cumin seeds.

Immerse the tuna in the marinade and store in the fridge for a few hours, turning several times.

When ready to cook, remove tuna from the marinade and heat a wok until it is evenly hot. Add a further smidgen of oil.

Sear the tuna in the hot wok over a high heat to form a crust and seal in the flavour. Sear on all sides but take care to keep the fish rare in the middle. Remove from heat and keep warm.

De-glaze the wok with the sherry and then add as much of the marinade as you need to make a sauce.

Bring to the boil and cook rapidly until the flavours have amalgamated and the liquor is syrupy.

Strain and whisk in a knob of butter.

Serve the tuna, sliced in half to show the rare middle, on a pile of noodles with the sauce poured over and around.

Top with a few slices of pickled ginger and some long chives.

# Aldo Zilli's
## Spaghetti with Fresh Lobster

Split lobster in half and break off claws. Remove the lobster meat, chop the body meat.

Place tomatoes in a bowl with parsley, basil and half the garlic, season with salt and pepper and set aside.

In a large frying pan heat half the oil, add onion and the rest of the garlic. Stir in the lobster meat and pour over the brandy and flambé. Once flames have died out add the tomato mixture with the wine. Turn down to a low heat and simmer for 5-8 minutes until the sauce has reduced slightly.

Cook the spaghetti as per pack instructions, drain.

Add spaghetti to lobster pan and toss well. Season to taste. Serve immediately and garnish with basil.

175g (6oz) spaghetti

sprigs of fresh basil to garnish

1 x 900g cooked lobster
(or two smaller ones)

2 beef tomatoes, skinned, seeded and chopped

4 tablespoons chopped fresh flat leaf parsley

4 tablespoons chopped fresh basil

2 garlic cloves, peeled and finely chopped

salt and freshly ground black pepper

50ml (2fl oz) olive oil

1 small red onion, peeled and finely chopped

50ml (2fl oz) brandy

150ml (5fl oz) dry white wine

# DELIA SMITH'S
## BLACKCURRANT CHEESECAKE

**SERVES 8-10**

1lb (450g) curd cheese
(or cottage cheese)
4 eggs (size 2)
1 teaspoon vanilla essence
5oz (150g) caster sugar
2 teaspoons lemon juice

Then for the base:
8 ginger biscuits
8 digestive biscuits
3oz (75g) butter
1 level teaspoon ground cinnamon

Then for the topping:
1lb (450g) blackcurrants, stripped
from the stalks
3-4 level tablespoons caster sugar
2 rounded teaspoons arrowroot

Pre-heat the oven to gas mark 3
(325°F) (170°C)
An 8½ inch (21.5cm) cake tin with a
loose base, lightly greased

*'The tart flavour of blackcurrants goes particularly well with the flavour of cream cheese, and this fairly large cheesecake will serve 8 or 10 people over a busy summer weekend.'*

Start by placing the cheese, eggs and sugar in a mixing bowl (if you're using cottage cheese, sieve it). Now, using preferably an electric hand whisk, whisk the mixture together till absolutely smooth. Then add the lemon juice and vanilla essence and mix again thoroughly. Now, melt the butter in a small saucepan; crush the biscuits to fine crumbs and mix them into the butter, adding the cinnamon.

Mix thoroughly with a fork, then press the biscuit mixture all over the base of the prepared tin as evenly as possible. Now pour the cheese mixture on top of the biscuit base and bake the cheesecake in the centre of the oven for about 30-40 minutes. Then turn the oven off, and leave the cheesecake in the warmth of the oven to finish cooking until the oven's cold.

To make the topping, wash the blackcurrants, then place them in a saucepan with the sugar and cook them very gently, without adding any water, until the juice runs out. Then in a small cup mix the arrowroot with a little cold water until smooth, pour this into the blackcurrant mixture and stir gently until the juices have come back to simmering point and the mixture has thickened.

Allow this to cool and spread it thickly over the top of the cheesecake after removing it from the tin.
If you like, you can press some more crushed biscuit crumbs round the side of the cheesecake. Then cover with an upturned basin and chill thoroughly before serving.

# GARY RHODES'
## BREAD AND BUTTER PUDDING

*'This is my all time favourite receipe - Bread and Butter Pudding which is always a great traditional family dessert. It brings back so many wonderful memories of when I was a child and is a pudding which I just love to share with many, many people.'*

Butter the bread. Split the vanilla pod and place in a saucepan with the cream and milk and bring to the boil. While it is heating, whisk together the egg yolks and caster sugar in a bowl. Allow the cream mix to cool a little, then strain it on to the egg yolks, stirring all the time. You now have the custard.

Cut the bread into triangular quarters or halves, and arrange in the dish in three layers, sprinkling the fruit between two layers and leaving the top clear. Now pour over the warm custard, lightly pressing the bread to help it soak in, and leave it to stand for a least 20-30 minutes before cooking to ensure that the bread absorbs all the custard.

The pudding can be prepared to this stage several hours in advance and cooked when needed. Place the dish in a roasting tray three-quarters filled with warm water and bake for 20-30 minutes until the pudding begins to set. Don't overcook it or the custard will scramble.

Remove the pudding from the water bath, sprinkle it liberally with caster sugar and glaze under the grill on a medium heat or with a gas gun to a crunchy golden finish. When glazing, the sugar dissolves and caramelises, and you may find that the corners of the bread begin to burn. This helps the flavour, giving a bittersweet taste that mellows when it is eaten with the rich custard, which seeps out of the wonderful bread sponge when you cut into it.

## SERVES 6-8

1 x 1.5-1.8 litre pudding
dish/basin buttered

12 medium slices white bread,
crusts cut off

50g unsalted butter, softened

1 vanilla pod or a few drops of
vanilla essence

300ml double cream

300ml milk

8 egg yolks

175g caster sugar, plus extra
for the caramelised topping

25g sultanas

25g raisins

Pre-heat the oven to
180°C/350°F/Gas mark 4

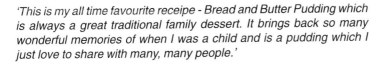

# LESLEY WATERS'
## CARAMELIZED SPICY FRUITS

1 large ripe mango
½ fresh ripe pineapple, cored,
peeled and thickly sliced
2 large bananas, peeled and
halved lengthways
1 ripe pawpaw, halved, seeded
and quartered

for the spicy butter:
85g (3oz) unsalted butter
5cm (2 inch) piece fresh root
ginger, finely chopped
2 teaspoons icing sugar
juice and grated zest of 1 lime

To prepare the mango, cut a thick slice from either side of the large flat stone that runs through the centre of the fruit. With a small, sharp knife, make diagonal cuts through the flesh, in a lattice fashion, taking great care not to cut through to the skin.

Cut each slice in half lengthways and push the skin up to open out the lattice cuts.

Preheat the grill to its highest setting and place the prepared fruits on to a baking tray, flesh side up. In a small saucepan, heat the butter until melted with the ginger and icing sugar. Stir in the lime juice and brush liberally over the fruits.

Grill the fruits for 6-7 minutes until caramelized and bubbling hot. Serve at once.

# LESLEY WATERS'
## COCONUT RICE

225g (8oz) Thai
fragrant rice, cooked
85g (3oz) sugar
1x 400g can coconut milk
1 cinnamon stick

Place the rice in a saucepan with the sugar, coconut milk and cinnamon stick.

Bring to the boil, cover and simmer for approx 10 minutes or until all the coconut milk has been absorbed.

To serve, allow the rice to cool before spooning into a pudding basin lined with cling film. Turn out and serve with the caramelized spicy fruits.

# ROZ DENNY'S
## PEAR FANS IN PEPPERCORN SYRUP

Dissolve the sugar in the water in a saucepan large enough to hold the pears, over a gentle heat and when completely clear, add the lemon peel and raise the heat and bubble for about 5 minutes.

Add the wine and spices. Return to a good boil and cook uncovered until the liquid is reduced down by a third.

Meanwhile, peel the pears with a swivel vegetable peeler, keeping the stalks on. Using a potato peeler or small sharp knife. Cut the base of the cores out in a cone and discard.

Place the pears in the syrup, rolling them to coat. Wet a large sheet of greaseproof paper and crumple up then place this on top of the pears. (Chefs call this a cartouche).

Bring the syrup to the boil, cover with the saucepan lid and lower the heat to a gentle simmer.

Cook for about 10 minutes, then uncover and turn the pears. Recover and continue poaching gently for another 10-15 minutes or until the fruits are tender.

Remove from the heat and cool the pears in the stock, and then press them well into the syrup and chill overnight. To serve, remove the pears and slash them from the base to the stalk end. Place on a plate and fan out.

Repeat with all the pears. Strain the syrup and serve with the pears. If you like a stronger syrup then simply boil it down again until reduced by a half.

Nice with ice cream.

## SERVES 6

100g sugar

150ml water and a strip of lemon peel

1 x 75cl bottle red wine

1/2 teaspoon black peppercorns

1 cinnamon stick

5 cardamom pods

1 star anise

6 firm pears, ideally squat shaped ones

RECIPES FROM THE FRONT LINE

# CHAPTER 2
# RECIPES FROM THE FRONT LINE OF ENTERTAINMENT AND THE MEDIA

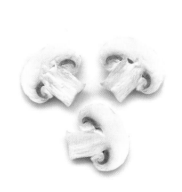  

# KATE ADIE'S
## GOAT A LA KURDISTAN

Find your goat. Not too easy when you're in a village in Kurdistan, following the end of the Gulf War. The village is deserted, the shop looted, only the occasional Iraqi policeman scuttles around. However, the priest in the next village has contacts.

Negotiate for goat. Clearly it has golden hooves and teeth of ivory, because it costeth a small fortune. But visiting journalists can't be choosers, and we've invited the Royal Marines to dinner.

Build barbecue. Those helpful people from the RAF airstrip at Sirsank 10 miles down the valley surely don't need every empty oil-drum in sight. Surely they wouldn't miss just one?

Nigel, our cameraman, constructs a mighty barbecue, tactfully concealing a number of official markings.

**Barbecuing the goat.**

Prepare vegetables. Clamber onto roof of fire station - next to which we sort of live - get satellite phone to work and order vegetables from neighbouring country, Turkey.

Fetch goat. Bit of a hiccup here. Brenda, our producer, cheerfully expected a neat sackful of jointed goat. Instead, a rather lively beast is blundering around in the back of her jeep.

Royal Marines offer to dispatch goat, but have to be dissuaded from machine-gun operation. We do not want to serve mince.

Do complex deal involving vegetables, wine and a helicopter off to Turkey. No further details available. Not officially, anyway, but it can be confirmed that people in uniform and journalists know that drink ought to be calculated not by bottle, but by hundredweight. Collect firewood, delicate sneaking operation, avoiding lurking Iraqi police.

Start cooking at sundown - goat not particularly youthful, by the look of it. Veggies have just hovered by.

Open wine, set out rickety table, salvaged from fire station. Borrow cutlery from Marine medical unit, open more wine. Arrival of guests. Open more wine. Our little village seems like a medieval fortress, with a small foreign force come to help the Kurds. We stand and stare at the magical valley in front of us. Think how lucky we are, open more wine, and savour roast goat.

# Dame Diana Rigg's
## ROAST LAMB AND FLAGEOLET BEANS

Roast lamb to taste - pink or whatever - salted, peppered, with a small handful of fresh rosemary. I always cover with foil until the last half hour when the garlic is thrown in.

When cooked, remove lamb from tin and keep warm. Remove as much fat as possible from roasting tin, add a little warm water, place over low heat and incorporate all the brown bits and juices. If necessary strain and return to tin.

Add both cans of flageolet beans but only the juice of one can. Stir until hot, then pour the lot around the lamb.

*'This sounds too easy to be true, but trust me it is delicious. The beans are infused with garlic and lamb juices and are delicious. You don't necessarily need potatoes with this, but lots of green vegetables or a huge green salad.'*

3-4lb leg of lamb

12-15 peeled garlic cloves

Rosemary

2 cans Flageolet beans

# LOYD GROSSMAN'S
## BROCCOLI AND CHILLI ORECCHIETTE

*'We eat a lot of pasta at home and one of our favourite recipes is for orecchiette with broccoli and chilli. Orecchiette are little 'ear shaped' pasta. Of course this recipe is good with other pasta shapes, but orecchiette are very typical of Apulia in Southern Italy, where this recipe and many others like it come from. This recipe is for two: my children aren't old enough to like this yet!'*

### METHOD:
Cook and drain some broccoli florets: use fresh, not frozen. Chop two or three cloves of garlic and soften them in some (about two tablespoons) of decent olive oil over a medium heat. Don't brown the garlic or else it will taste bitter.

Lower the heat a bit and add six to eight tinned anchovy fillets, mash them with a wooden spoon and keep cooking until they dissolve into a paste.

Then add two dried red chillies and the broccoli florets, and keep this mixture over a very low flame whilst you boil your pasta. Drain the pasta, pour the sauce over it and eat with gusto.

*Strictly speaking you shouldn't add grated Parmesan cheese, but I do. Serve it with a green salad and you've got a splendid supper.*

# ANTHEA TURNER'S
## SMOKED FISH PIE

Arrange fish in a baking tin, pour half the milk over it, add a few flecks of the butter and the bay leaf, then bake in the oven for 15-20 minutes. Pour off and reserve the cooking liquid, then remove the skin from the fish and flake the flesh into largish pieces.

Next make the sauce by melting the remaining butter in a saucepan, then stir in the flour and gradually add the fish liquid bit by bit, stirring well after each addition.

When all the liquid is in, finish the sauce by gradually adding the remaining milk, seasoning with salt and pepper and simmer for 3-4 minutes.

Now mix the fish into the sauce, together with the hard-boiled eggs, parsley and capers, then taste to see if it needs any more seasoning and stir in the lemon juice. Pour the mixture into a buttered baking dish (about 2½ pints).

Next prepare the topping. Cream the potatoes, starting off with a large fork, then finishing off with an electric beater if you have one, adding the butter and milk. Season the potatoes with salt and pepper and add some freshly grated nutmeg, spread evenly all over the fish then sprinkle the cheese all over.

Bake on a high shelf in the oven, still at gas mark 6, 400°F (200°C) for about 30 minutes, by which time the pie will be heated through and the top will be nicely brown.

### SERVES 4

1½lb (700g) smoked haddock

4 kipper fillets, weighing a total
4-6oz (110-175g)

1 pint  (570ml) milk

4oz (110g)  butter

1 bay leaf

2oz (50g) flour

2 hard-boiled eggs,
 roughly chopped

3 tablespoons fresh
chopped parsley

1 tablespoon capers
(can be left out if unavailable)

1 tablespoon lemon juice

salt and freshly milled black pepper

for the topping:

2lb (900g) fresh boiled potatoes

2oz (50g) butter

4 tablespoons milk

freshly grated nutmeg

1oz (25g) strong
cheddar cheese, grated

Pre-heat the oven
to 400°F (200°C) or gas mark 6

# Phillip Schofield's
## POTATO CAKES

Peel and boil sufficient potatoes for the amount of people needed. When cooked, mash in the usual way with lots of milk and butter and salt to taste.

Add enough self-raising flour to make into a stiff dough. Roll out on a floured board into individual circles about 5 inches across and 1/2 inch deep.

Cook near the top of a hot oven for about 15-20 minutes until golden brown.

Butter and eat immediately!

# LENNY HENRY'S
## KILLER CHILLI RECIPE

*'Place rabbit's foot around your neck (you're going to need all the luck you can get because I certainly don't know what I'm doing!).'*

Chop onions and green peppers. Fry in about 4oz butter until they are fairly translucent (that means see-through, thicky). Add the meat and fry until it is brown.

Add the tomatoes and stir for a couple of minutes until they are bubbling noisily. Add tomato purée (about 1 tablespoon) and stir until sauce thickens. Add all the spices and herbs, chop mushrooms, add them and stir for 2 minutes.

Add kidney beans and give it a good stir. Add a dash of Tabasco and crumble in Oxo cubes and wine and stir again.

Put on a low heat, eg gas mark 2, and simmer for about one hour stirring occasionally. After this time it should be a lovely dark brown colour and quite thick. If there is a layer of fat on top, scrape off with a spoon.

*'Yum, yum in my tum!'*

Serve with rice or pitta bread to about 4 people.

**SERVES 4**

1lb minced beef
2 big onions
2 green peppers
1 tin Italian tomatoes
1 tin kidney beans
tomato purée
Chilli powder (mild or not depending on whether your tongue is made of leather!)
pinch of oregano
pinch of mixed spices
pinch of cloves
dash of Tabasco
glass of red wine
2 beef Oxo cubes
¼lb mushrooms
lucky Rabbit's foot!

# Ewan McGregor
## 'Eat up, ye'r at yer aunties!'
## Braised Beef in Guinness

**SERVES 6-8**

3lb brisket of beef cut
into 2 inch cubes

2 tablespoons of olive oil

8oz onions quartered and
separated into layers

1 well heaped tablespoon
plain flour

6 pints of Guinness

fresh thyme

1 bay leaf

1 large clove of garlic, crushed

salt and pepper

Pre-heat oven to 275°F (140°C) or
gas mark 1

*'I've recently spent a lot of time filming in Ireland, so my recipe has a distinctly Irish flavour. The good thing about this recipe is if you are in a hurry and don't have the time required to cook this dish (as it does take some time) then ignore all the ingredients bar one: the Guinness. You will still be left with a wholesome meal full of goodness that will have you coming back for more!'*

Heat the oil in a large flame proof casserole dish and, when hot, add the meat a few pieces at a time. Sear them until they are nice and brown. Remove onto a plate then add the onions and cook until brown at the edges.

Lower the heat and return the meat to the casserole (together with any juices on the plate), then stir in the flour using a wooden spoon.

Now stir in 1 pint of the Guinness and add the thyme, bay leaf and garlic. Season with salt and pepper and bring the whole lot slowly up to simmering point.

Cover the casserole and transfer to the preheated oven. Cook for 3 hours. Don't be tempted to try it half way through because the beer needs time to transform itself into a delicious sauce.

While the dish is in the oven, drink the remainder of the Guinness! Serve with creamy mashed Irish potatoes and loads of fresh veg.

# TIM VINCENT'S
## FAVOURITE PASTA DISH

Boil the pasta.

Fry up the vegetables and add Dolmio and garlic. Heat up to a nice sauce, which should take about 5-6 minutes. Add the salami last.

Pour the sauce over the pasta and add slices of Red Leicester cheese on the top. Melt it under a grill.

pasta twirls

Dolmio

fresh vegetables - such as green and yellow peppers,

onion and mushrooms

garlic

herbs - such as oregano and basil etc

salami

Red Leicester cheese

# THE RED ARROWS

### RECIPE FOR SUCCESS

The Red Arrows display is the end result of around five months of training, flying three times a day, until the show is of a consistently high standard to be considered fit for the public. Although the show will hopefully appear near perfect to the crowd, the team is constantly trying to refine and improve throughout the summer season, and every show is debriefed to try and improve for the next one. The sort of errors and changes discussed in the debrief often only amount to a position change of a foot or two, but it is only by striving for perfection that standards are maintained.

The key to flying the show is to fly smoothly. Although it is probably possible to stay in more or less the right place whilst thrashing the flying controls around, the people flying around you will not thank you for it. It is better to be out of position for several seconds and slowly correct back to the right position, than to see an error and attempt to instantly correct it. Allied to smoothness is the reliance on the radio. All moves and changes of any sort are called on the radio, normally by the leader. He will attempt to be consistent in his cadence in every show. In that way, when he calls, for instance, that he is turning, everybody will start turning on his call, rather than waiting to see his aircraft move. In this way, any lag, or reaction time, is reduced to a minimum and ideally zero.

*'On two occasions during the second half, all the aircraft split off separately and the rejoins are as difficult and important as anything the crowd see in the display.'*

The 2000 show starts by running in from behind the right-hand side of the crowd. Rules now prohibit overflight of the crowd, which was, for a long time, how the show started. During the first half, all nine aircraft stay together in close formation. In this period, flying smoothly is particularly important, although it is important to try and maintain the same standard even when not right in front of the crowd (known as link flying). There are low and high (known as 'flat' and 'full') variations of every manoeuvre, and each show will vary, primarily according to the height of the cloudbase. It is possible to change from full to flat and back again during a display, due to changing weather conditions. At the end of the first half, the nine jets split into a five and a four. The five are called 'Enid' (the famous five) and are generally the less experienced team members. The four are 'Gypo' and include the synchro pair, who perform the opposition passes. The second half contains more dynamic manoeuvring by all the aircraft, although the same principles apply in achieving a high standard. On two occasions during the second half, all the aircraft split off separately and the rejoins are as difficult and important as anything the crowd see in the display. At the end of the show, the team are all split and must join together quickly for the landing. There is no time to relax until all aircraft are on chocks, since just landing and taxiing nine aircraft together requires full concentration. Then it's off to the debrief before we go and do it all again.

BY FLT LT J HUGHES BSc RAF
RED 3 OF THE RED ARROWS BASED AT RAF CRANWELL.

RECIPES FROM THE FRONT LINE

# Caf's Curry
## aka Chicken Tikka Masala
### by Caf Hawker (wife of red 2)

**Serves 4**

Firstly you need to marinade your chicken. The longer the better, I try to do it for at least 24hrs. This is for about ½lb chicken.

Chuck all the marinade ingredients in a food processor and blend until smooth-ish and then pour over the chicken and leave to marinade between 6-30 hours.

Take the marinading chicken and either barbecue, stir fry, or grill for 15 mins, or over bake for 15-20 mins on 160°C/325°F, gas mark 3.

For the sauce, heat the ghee, add paste, marinade and puree and simmer for about 2 mins. Then add pepper, chillies, tomatoes and again simmer for 5 mins. Add the rest of the ingredients, mix and allow to simmer for a further few mins, then add the chicken and serve when hot.

I tend to add onions, and usually end up adding the whole tub of cream and have also been known to add half a block of creamed coconut, all of which seem to make it lovely! I'm often led by how much there seems to be in the wok, who is coming to eat with us and how much I want left over!

The Reds do like this recipe and if there are any left overs they are taken into the crew room the next day and will readily be eaten cold on a piece of bread. For those more cultured than the boys, it tastes equally as nice with pitta bread and salad!

For the marinade:

5oz natural yoghurt

3 tablespoons mustard (I tend to use Colmans mustard or such like)

2 tablespoons lemon juice

1teaspoon of garlic purée (or a few cloves)

1 teaspoon of ginger puree (or about an inch or so of stem ginger peeled and chopped)

2 green chillies (seeds in or out depending on heat required)

1 teaspoon of bottled mint (stuff used for roasts)

3 tablespoons fresh coriander

1 teaspoon cumin

1 teaspoon of garam masala

2 tablespoons tandoori/tikka paste/dry mix (I tend to use paste)

1 teaspoon of salt

For the Chicken Tikka Masala sauce:

Marinading chicken approx 1½lbs

3 teaspoons vegetable oil or ghee

2 teaspoons tandoori paste

2 tablespoons tandoori marinade (as above)

2 teaspoons tomato purée

½ green pepper

1-4 green chillies (again depending on heat required)

1 tomato chopped

2 tablespoons natural yoghurt/ fromage frais

2 tablespoons fresh coriander

1 tablespoon ground almonds

1 tablespoon single cream

salt to taste

# MR BEAN'S (ROWAN ATKINSON)
## BAKED BEANS

1 can of baked beans
toast

Heat the beans in a pan until they go all bubbly.

Pour over toast and serve.

# MARTIN CLUNE'S
## AND MA CLUNE'S FISH SQUAG

1lb un-peeled prawns
¹/₂lb cod (Coley will do)
2oz long grain rice (approx)
¹/₄ pt thick mayonnaise
(preferably home made!)
2 teaspoons gelatin
Anchovy essence

Coarsely chop prawns reserving some for decoration. Boil the prawn shells hard and then process them. Strain and use the liquid to cook the fish, and then the rice in the same stock. Dissolve the gelatin in some of the same stock.

Mix rice, fish, prawns, mayonnaise and gelatin. Flavour to taste with salt, pepper and anchovy essence. Put in individual ramekins to set, or one large dish. Turn out and decorate with whole prawns.

*'None of these measurements have to be exact - the more prawns the better!'*

# KATE WINSLET'S
## BANANA AND WALNUT LOAF

*'I recommend organic bananas simply because they taste so lovely, but ordinary bananas will of course do just as well!'*

Cream together the margarine and sugar until light and soft. In a separate bowl, mash the bananas and then mix them in with the sugar and margarine.

Break the eggs into the mixture and beat these in well with a wooden spoon, (the mixture will look a bit runny at this stage - this is supposed to happen!).

Carefully fold in the sifted flour and then the chopped walnuts. This is where you can add the milk if the mixture looks a little dry (this is most often the case if the bananas aren't very ripe).

Turn the mixture into a greased 1kg loaf tin (it is a good idea to line the tin as well if you have time) and bake in the oven for 1 hour. Leave to cool in the tin for approximately 5 minutes and then turn out onto a wire rack.

4oz (100g) soft margarine

6oz (175g) light muscovado sugar

2 ripe organic bananas

2 eggs

8oz (225g) self raising flour

2oz (50g) chopped walnuts

2 tablespoons milk (optional)

Pre-heat the oven to 180°C (350°F) or Gas Mark 4

# ZOE BALL'S
## RICH CHOCOLATE MOUSSE

**SERVES 4**

8oz (225g) plain chocolate, broken into pieces

4 eggs separated

1 tablespoon rum, brandy or orange juice

½ oz (15g) butter

Melt the chocolate in a double boiler or in a basin over hot water. When melted stir in, one at a time, the egg yolks, rum and butter.

Whisk the egg whites in a clean bowl until stiff and fold them into the chocolate mixture until thoroughly mixed.

To freeze: Spoon into four small dishes, cover, seal and freeze. To serve: Thaw in the refrigerator for 2-3 hours and serve chilled, decorated with whipped cream.

# SIR CLIFF RICHARD'S
## TRANSKEI MUD

Preparation time: 20 minutes. Cooking time: 2 hours, plus overnight cooling for condensed milk, and overnight refrigeration for pudding.

Boil the can of condensed milk unopened, and completely covered with water at all times, for about two hours. Allow it to cool fully - or overnight.

Whisk the double cream until it stands in soft peaks. Slowly add the caramelised milk, one spoonful at a time. Mix thoroughly.

Grate all the chocolate, then, reserving a little for decoration, add it to the mixture and stir in.

Layer the mixture into a glass serving dish, alternating with the digestive biscuits, making three layers of each. Refrigerate overnight. Sprinkle over the remaining chocolate before serving.

*'If I'm feeling particularly indulgent, I whip a second carton of double cream until stiff, and spread this over the pudding before decorating with remaining chocolate!'*

Serve in small portions as the pudding is very rich.

### SERVES 8

405g can of condensed milk

284ml carton double cream

200g digestive biscuits, crushed

100g mint chocolate

(such as Aero), grated

# EMMA FORBES'
## CHOCOLATE FRIDGE CAKE

8oz (225g) plain chocolate
1oz (25g) Demerara sugar
4oz (100g) butter
2 tablespoons golden syrup
450g plain, sweet biscuits
(such as Rich Tea)
1 packet of peanuts and raisins
(unsalted)

In a bowl suspended over a pan of gently simmering water, put the chocolate, sugar, butter and syrup and melt them together.

In another bowl, break up the biscuits into small bits and add all the peanuts and raisins.

Pour the melted mixture over the biscuits, nuts and raisins and stir really well. Pour into a greased 20cm/8 inch square cake tin. Using a wooden spoon, press the mixture firmly down, then leave in the fridge until set.

You could add your choice of ingredients to this, such as chopped marshmallows or mixed nuts, or you could experiment using different kinds of biscuits.

*'Remember to serve only small pieces as it is incredibly sickly. To decorate the cake, you can grate some extra chocolate over the top or dust it lightly with a little icing sugar.'*

# MICHAEL BARRYMORE'S
## HOT FUDGE SAUCE

Place all the ingredients in a small, strong saucepan, and heat gently for about 5 minutes until they are well blended together. Do not boil.

Serve on top of ice cream, straight from the pan!

3oz soft brown sugar

2 level tablespoons golden syrup

1oz margarine

4 tablespoons unsweetened evaporated milk

# COCKTAILS:
## SANDRINGHAM ESTATE OFFICE'S GAME KEEPERS HAT

### CHAMPAGNE BRAMBLE LIQUEUR

To make this delightfully refreshing cocktail, just add one part Bramble liqueur to a champagne flute and top up with six parts champagne or sparkling wine.

*Then, just sit back and relax!*

RECIPES FROM THE FRONT LINE

# CHAPTER THREE
## RECIPES FROM THE FRONT LINE
### OF YESTERDAY'S ROYAL AIR FORCE
#### IN WORLD WAR TWO
##### BY KEN DELVE
###### MANAGING EDITOR *FLYPAST* MAGAZINE

SELETAR     SINGAPORE

RAF

1940
Christmas

MENU
Cream of Tomato Soup
Roast Turkey, Roast Pork,
Sausage Stuffing
New Potatoes, Potato Rolls
Brussel Sprouts, Cauliflower

Xmas Pudding,
Mince Pies, Brandy Sauce

Pears, Apples, Oranges Nuts

Beer, Minerals
Cigarettes

B.M.LECK.

# THE RAF AT WAR 1939-45

One of the most famous of military maxims is that 'an army marches on its stomach', meaning that as long as the troops have regular and reasonable food, then they will be able to perform their duties in an appropriate fashion - and by implication without such supplies of food the reverse would be true. For the RAF in World War Two food supplies were often a problem in various overseas theatres of operation: the aerial siege of Malta in 1941-42, for example, meant that the whole island, and the RAF personnel who lived and worked at the three airfields and other installations, suffered severe shortages of food, especially fresh food. Indeed, lack of fresh food is the most consistent comment from RAF veterans of this period; the ubiquitous dried (powdered egg being the most notable) and tinned foods may well have provided the staple requirements in terms of nutrition but were hardly the stuff of gourmet meals!

Rationing began in 1940 - and remained in place until 1954. Instant coffee was introduced in 1939, bad timing as war broke out the same year, although the two events are not usually seen to be connected!

The RAF was short of experienced personnel and in its search for catering staff stated that, 'cooks must be accustomed to dealing with large numbers. Restaurant, hotel or catering cooks are admirable for this work.' Ladies were recruited into the WAAF as cooks in Trade Group 3 (which included fabric workers and shoe repairers) but the majority of catering staff were male.

Most RAF personnel have few recollections of particular dishes that either they missed during the war or ones that they have fond memories of; food was simply not high on the list of concerns for most of them - except on odd occasions. Many of the recipes shown here were not

*'Instant coffee was introduced in 1939, bad timing as war broke out the same year, although the two events are not usually seen to be connected!'*

solely applicable to the RAF but are rather more indicative of wartime Britain in general.

RAF personnel were deployed in all the war's operational theatres - from Europe to the baking (but sometimes wet and cold) deserts of North Africa, from the malarial conditions of West Africa to the jungles of the Far East; between each theatre conditions varied greatly and those in the Home Commands, operating out of the UK, generally had the better living conditions - and catering. In the Western Desert campaigns, the front lines were very fluid and airfields were often little more than areas of desert with groups of tents, although there were a number of more permanent facilities, especially those in the RAF's rear areas in Egypt. The abiding memory of those who served in the desert was not so much of any particular food but rather of the swarms of flies and the amount of sand that did their best to contaminate anything that was on offer.

UK-based RAF personnel seemed to spend a great deal of their off-duty time at public houses and each squadron tended to have its own favourite watering hole - the aircrew and groundcrew favouring different locations. Beer was central to much of the RAF's recreational activity (just as it is today!) and this was equally true of the UK and overseas. Indeed, the need to acquire supplies of beer when outside of the UK taxed many an RAF unit and there are instances of squadrons adapting underwing pylons on aircraft so that they could carry barrels of beer. A visit to the local pub also provided the opportunity for a pie, the nature of which depended on the part of the country - each region having its own specialities - and, as always, the availability of ingredients. Game pies were popular, the meat element of which might be rabbit, pigeon or pheasant acquired without too many questions being asked!

*'The abiding memory of those who served in the desert was not so much of any particular food but rather of the swarms of flies and the amount of sand that did their best to contaminate anything that was on offer.'*

**The beer bottles are perhaps the most significant element of this photograph showing 'Mosquito crew relaxing'.**

**Crews of 55 Squadron in the mess tent at Cecina, 1944.**

# PIGEON PIE

As with most pies the exact nature of the dish is variable, especially during the war when some of the items in a 'classic' pigeon pie might well have been replaced by other more readily available ingredients. For many pub pies the addition of beer was a frequent one. The following is a more traditional pigeon pie recipe:

Line a dish with the pastry, add the pigeon, bacon and shallots. Add the salt/pepper and the parsley, followed by the stock. Place a pie funnel in the centre and cover all with a pastry top, cutting a hole for the funnel. Decorate the edges of the pie and glaze with egg wash. Bake for 1½ hours at 350°F.

Of the official meats, corned beef was one of the commonest and between 1939 and 1945 a great many dishes were devised to make best use of - some would say disguise - this ubiquitous product. It became a substance you either liked or hated - not that it made much difference as often there was little else.

8 rashers of bacon (probably omitted)

4 shallot cloves, chopped

2 pigeons, cut into quarters or pieces

pinch of pepper and salt

4 tablespoons of parsley

3 cups of strong stock

pastry to line dish and cover pie

# Corned Beef Pie

3 rations of corned beef

1 cup finely shredded
vegetables

1 Oxo cube

1 teaspoonful of chopped
parsley

piece of lard

1 dessertspoon of flour

sufficient shortcrust pastry
for a pie dish

Along with Ministry of Food advice pamphlets, food manufacturers also issued recipe ideas, the following one coming from a 1942 suggestion by Oxo.

Melt fat in a pan and add the shredded vegetables, stir in the flour and cook for a few minutes. Add one cup of cold water and the Oxo cube (crumbled), stir until the mixture thickens. Add cubed meat, parsley and salt/pepper as required. Line a small plate or pie dish with pastry and add the meat mixture, cover with pastry. Bake in moderate oven for 30 minutes.

'Tea and a wad' was the cry of almost every British soldier and airman during the war and these delights were usually provided by the ever-present, and greatly appreciated, NAAFI (Navy, Army, Air Force Institute) wagon. The 'wad' was a sandwich of often epic proportions in terms of the thickness of the slices of bread, the contents of the sandwich being variable, although corned beef (a staple of much of wartime Britain) was one of the common fillings.

**A 149 Squadron crew at the post-mission debrief - note the cups of tea and plate of sandwiches.**

Recipes from the Front Line

**Stocking up with sweets and supplies at the NAAFI.**

# DRINKS

Tea was the most popular of drinks and was usually made strong, partly to disguise the use of dried milk.  Instructions were provided as to how to prepare liquid milk from the powdered substance:

3 tablespoons (2oz) of dried milk
2 breakfast cups of water
Mix the dried milk with 2 tablespoons of the water and beat very hard with a wooden spoon or a whisk until smooth. Add the rest of the water gradually and stir or whisk well.

Instructions were also issued as to how to make cocoa with dried milk:
3 tablespoons of dried milk
2 breakfast cups water
cocoa powder
Mix the milk powder with the cocoa powder, stir in the boiling water gradually until smooth, boil for one minute.

Dried milk was also used in various soups, including one that was known as 'Two Minute Soup':
4 tablespoons of dried milk
2 breakfast-cups of water
1 teaspoon vegetable or meat extract
or 2 tablespoons chopped parsley and a pinch of salt
Mix the milk with some of the water to form liquid milk, bring to the boil and stir in the extract or the parsley and salt.

# CAKES

Luxuries such as cakes were not altogether forgotten, although they were certainly rare everywhere except in the UK or except on special occasions.  There are various recipes that have been recalled by RAF veterans, although these are usually based on cakes that were no longer available to them rather than those that they remember from the war - although rock cakes bought at the NAAFI crop up in conversation more often than any other cake type.

## ROCK CAKES

8oz self-raising flour
teaspoon salt
pinch of mixed spice
3oz butter
3oz caster sugar
3oz sultanas
1 large egg
2 tablespoons milk
Demerara sugar

I have not been able to uncover the NAAFI rock cake recipe, perhaps just as well (!) but the following is a fairly typical recipe, although the exact constituents may have varied depending on what was available - according to one RAF chef of the period anything was available as long as you had the right 'Spiv' contact and were able to trade material, perhaps silk from parachutes. This was not perhaps encouraged and certainly not officially sanctioned but it did take place.

Put sifted flour, salt and mixed spice in a basin and add the butter - cut in pieces - rubbing this into the flour mix. Add the sugar and sultanas and mix. Mix the egg and milk and add to the other ingredients, using a fork to mix the rough dough to achieve fairly firm dough.

Pile the mixture into 12 rough heaps on greased baking trays and sprinkle a little Demerara sugar on top of each one. Bake in hot oven 200°C/Gas 6 for about 15-20 minutes.

## WELSH GRIDDLE CAKES

8oz plain white flour
8oz plain wholemeal flour
tablespoon baking powder
pinch of salt
4oz butter
4oz lard
4oz currants
1 teaspoon mixed spice
6oz sugar
1 egg
2 tablespoons milk

This recipe was provided by a man who recalls that it was popular in much of Wales from before the war and that at certain RAF stations, either those in Wales or those with cooks with Welsh roots, it was readily available - although again the exact ingredients might vary with availability.

Mix the flour, salt and baking powder and crumble in the butter and lard. Add the sugar, currants and mixed spice. Add the beaten egg and milk and mix. Roll out and cut with a tumbler. Bake on griddle and add a dusting of caster sugar.

## IN THE SERVICES

'It was, of course, very different for Service personnel. On reporting for duty (at Lords Cricket Ground!) we were given a taste of the culinary delights provided by the cooks who had probably been bank clerks or bus conductors a few months earlier.

Sausage and mash was almost a staple diet until flying training eventually began. The best food in the world at that time was the wonderful Welsh Rarebits available in the NAAFI. I was lucky to go to the RAF College at Cranwell for my Service Flying Training and here we were treated, as cadets, with food every day that our parents at home would be unable to get more than once a week. We heard that

Two RAF chefs pose at a formal function, the selection of dishes appear to be sweets and cakes but unfortunately there are no details.

aircrews on ops always got eggs and bacon but so did we as trainee pilots.

After getting my wings I was posted to the Middle East and this broadened our experience considerably. On the ship (Capetown Castle) taking us to Port Said - a long voyage so as to avoid enemy submarines, we took a circuitous route and at one time were only a day's sailing from New York! - we enjoyed such things as bread-rolls freshly baked on board and the luxury of regular meal times sitting at tables with brilliant white cloths. In Egypt we had as much fresh fruit as we wanted. I remember that we were supplied with bunches of bananas by the Sudanese Mess staff for which the going rate was two cigarettes! Flying from Palestine we saw acres of orange groves and in Jaffa at one time there were mountains of oranges going to waste because there were no ships to export them.

On leave in Cairo it was almost obligatory to take tea at the Greek café Groppi's and indulge in 'sticky cakes' the like of which we had not seen in the UK for a long time.

In Italy it was different altogether. We were dependent on our basic service rations and were always on the lookout for ways of augmenting them. Eggs from local farmers were a luxury and before parting with any, the farmers had to be convinced it was not us who had bombed them before the last advance! One thing we were never short of in Italy was the opportunity to taste good wines and when the fighting finished hidden stocks came to light everywhere. In Austria there was no vine but schnapps to toast our success and plenty of dairy produce to supply the Mess.' (From Vivian A Salter).

These were the days of strict rationing, when everyone not in the Armed Forces was encouraged to *Dig for Victory* and grow vegetables and other produce in their gardens and allotments. Lawns and flower-beds were turned into vegetable gardens and office workers cultivated plots in town parks. The aim was to make Britain as self-sufficient in food as possible. To this end chickens, rabbits, and even pigs ware

*'...we enjoyed such things as bread-rolls freshly baked on board and the luxury of regular meal times sitting at tables with brilliant white cloths.'*

reared in town gardens.

From the beginning of 1940 rationing was introduced: 4 oz of bacon and butter, and 12 oz of sugar was allowed per person per week. Meat rationing followed - by price, ie more of a cheap cut could be purchased - and later the rationing system was extended to include cooking fats, jam, cheese, tea, eggs and milk. One egg was permitted every two weeks and even that depended on a supply being available! Also, a points system was introduced to cover other foods such as cereals, canned goods, fruit, biscuits and fish. These were all 'valued' at a particular number of points and could be bought up to the limit of points each customer had… usually not many!

'British Restaurants' were set up where workers could get a cheap simple meal and a small portion of minced meat with potato, carrots and parsnips would be typical. The Government issued for school children a daily allocation of milk, orange juice and cod liver oil to ensure they had sufficient vitamins.

There was a great deal of propaganda with the Government issuing suggested recipes encouraging people to eat more available vegetables and using such figures as Potato Pete and Doctor Carrot to get the message across.

*'The aim was to make Britain as self-sufficient in food as possible. To this end chickens, rabbits, and even pigs were reared in town gardens.'*

TYPICAL OF THESE RECIPES:

## CARROT CROQUETTES

6 carrots
1oz margarine
oatmeal
1 gill of milk
1oz cornflour
fat for frying and
seasoning to taste

Boil the carrots until tender, drain and mash or sieve. Add seasoning. Make a thick white sauce with the milk margarine and cornflour and add the carrot to it. When the mixture is cold, shape into croquettes and roll in the oatmeal. Fry in deep hot fat, drain and serve.

## WAR AND PEACE PUDDING

Take a cup of flour, half a cup of suet, half a cup of dried fruit, a cupful of bread crumbs and some mixed spice to taste. Add a whole cup of grated raw carrot with a teaspoon of bicarbonate of soda dissolved in a little water. Mix thoroughly and put in a greased pudding bowl, then boil or steam for about two or three hours.

**Crews of a Boston squadron collect their rations.**

RECIPES FROM THE FRONT LINE

These aircrew of 58 Squadron at Linton-on-Ouse in 1940 look well fed - but there was another 5 years of war to go.

## MEXICAN CREAM

Mix the dry ingredients together and to a smooth paste with a little coffee. Boil the remaining coffee and pour over the other ingredients and return to the heat and boil for a further three minutes. Add the vanilla essence and pour into separate serving dishes. Serve when completely cold.

*The dried egg powder was an American invention which, poured into a hot frying pan, swelled alarmingly but made a good breakfast! People became accustomed to both dried milk and dried egg. A packet of dried egg was about equal to a dozen eggs and one was allowed per person every two months - if available.

2 teaspoons of dried egg powder *
2 tablespoons of flour
3 tablespoons of cocoa
3 tablespoons of sugar
a pint of black coffee
vanilla essence
a pinch of salt to taste

Cakes were often made with potato. There was a Woolton Pie - a horrible concoction of potatoes, parsnips and herbs, 'Mashed bananas' for children were made with cooked bread mashed with parsnips, a little sugar, and a drop or two of essence of banana! Many young children never saw a real banana and when they eventually became available again it must have been a pleasant surprise.

# COASTAL COMMAND - FLYING BOATS

The RAF's long-range maritime patrol flying boats such as the Short Sunderland and Consolidated Catalina flew some of the longest sorties of the war - anything up to 20 hours patrolling vast areas of ocean. In order to keep alert for such a long period of time, looking for signs of any enemy submarines, the crew were provided with a substantial pack-up of food for each sortie, and as each aircraft had its own galley then hot food was very much the order of the day. According to one

RAF record a typical menu for a long maritime patrol might be:
**Breakfast:** cereal, bacon and sausage, tea, bread and butter.
**Lunch:** soup, half the quantity of steak carried in store, cubed and stewed, potatoes and vegetables, dried fruit, orange.
**Tea:** poached or scrambled egg, bread and butter, tea.
**Supper:** Remainder of steak fried, potatoes and vegetables, bread and butter with cheese.

Between the four hot meals chocolate and barley sugar were eaten, and cocoa, tea or other hot drinks provided - so that the crew could eat or drink something every two hours.

# BOMBER COMMAND

Whilst the crews of Coastal Command flew the longest sorties and had the luxury of an on-board galley that meant they were able to enjoy an impressive in-flight catering routine, for the crews of the RAF's heavy bombers the situation was somewhat more basic. The majority of attacks by RAF Bomber Command from 1941 to early 1945 were made at night, with targets as far afield as eastern Germany involving long night flights. Unlike the coastal crews, the crews of the Lancasters, Stirlings and Halifaxes had no way of preparing hot food - the best they could do was to take along a Thermos of hot drink - soup, coffee or cocoa being the normal beverage options. The reliability of the Thermos flask was aptly demonstrated when a Halifax of 35 Squadron was recovered from a Norwegian lake some 50 years after it had been shot down. The Thermos was still in the rear turret, with liquid - but not hot!

When crews had completed their planning for the night's mission there was usually time for a hot meal in their respective messes before having to pick up their kit and make their way to the aircraft dispersals. Rations were picked up for the flight, usually consisting of biscuits, apple/orange, chocolate, barley sugar (one of the favourite items), chewing gum and raisins.

'The best thing about night flying was the rare treat of bacon and eggs,' recalled Ron Waite in his biography 'Death or Decoration' (Newton, 1991). 'Sitting at one of the 12-foot long tables I had scarcely to wait 5 minutes when a comfortably-built WAAF came in carrying a large plate. '

**Lancaster flown by John Carsons and crew dropping food supplies to Dutch civilians during operation Manna.**

RECIPES FROM THE FRONT LINE

'There you are Sir. Supposed to be only one rasher and one egg really.'

'I gazed at the feast of two back rashers, an egg and two deliciously obese sausages. A couple of rounds of toast, marmalade and a strong, hot sweet tea completed the repast.' Having landed from a raid, the first duty of the crews was to go through debriefing with the intelligence section - and take the opportunity for a hot drink of tea or cocoa and a sandwich, as evidenced in many photographs of such debriefs.

The opportunity to visit local hostelries - other than pubs - was also taken whenever possible, most officers frequenting restaurants from time to time, especially when within range of London, where shortages never seemed to be a major problem (an active band of Spivs no doubt). Cafés were equally popular and some, such as Betty's Bar in York, became famous for their 'role' in the war; indeed, Betty's is still trading on that connection and the mirror signed by wartime aircrew is now a tourist attraction at the café. There were certainly advantages to being based in the UK!

# DON BENNETT'S CHOCOLATE CAKE

'Every night of his life the only 'pudding' Pathfinder Don Bennett ever wanted was his wife, Ly's, famous chocolate cake with lashings of cream!' (From Noreen Cooper, Bennett's daughter)

Blend the sugar and butter together in a mixer. Add one egg after another into the mixer, blend. Then add the flour and dry ingredients, blend again and finally add the milk, mix again until combined.
Place mixture in a greased cake tin and bake for one hour in a moderate oven (160°C-180°C).

For the icing:
Mix together well, 1/2lb of icing sugar with 2 tablespoons of cocoa powder. Add 1oz butter and 2 tablespoons of Lyles Golden Syrup and mix again. Add only a little hot water to make the icing of spreading consistency.

Cut the cooled cake in two halves and spread the icing between the layers and on top.

4 eggs
6oz sugar
8oz butter
12oz self-raising flour
cup Lyles Golden Syrup
pinch of salt
1/2oz bicarbonate of soda
2-3 tablespoons of cocoa powder
cup or less milk

Air Vice Marshal Donald (Don) Bennett played a central role in RAF Bomber Command as the mastermind behind and commander of the Pathfinder Force (PFF) which from its creation in 1942 helped to make Bomber Command into an effective offensive force. Born in Queensland, Australia, in 1910 he joined the Royal Australian Air Force in 1930 and was sent to England to complete his training, joining No 29 Squadron with its Siskin fighters. He subsequently served with a flying boat squadron and with Imperial Airways, rejoining the RAF in 1941 and taking command of No 77 Squadron, Bomber Command. After serving as Commanding Officer of No 10 Squadron he was promoted to Group Captain and given the task of organising the new specialist force, under the designation No 8 Group (from 1943 with Bennett becoming its Air Commodore).

# OVERSEAS

**July 1943, Benina, Libya - the mess hall and kitchens; although this shows mainly American personnel the airfield was also used by the RAF.**

As mentioned in the introductory section, conditions were far worse at the RAF's overseas bases, particularly in the deserts and jungles. 'The cookhouse staff worked under very difficult conditions, entirely in the open, making the best of a bad job with basic rations and waging a constant battle with flies.' So recalled Vivian Jacobs in his autobiography 'The Woodpecker Story - 136 Squadron' (Pentland Press 1994). 'The MO was reported as having advised someone suffering from stomach trouble, desperate for a cure by that stage, that the only cure was to shoot the cook! In desperation, some of the airmen formed a little consortium and set out to provide their own evening meals. There was a native fireplace in one of the mud huts so they bought a tin of ghee (clarified butter) in town and either bought or 'acquired' eggs, bacon, bread, tomatoes and anything else they could scrounge from the cookhouse to provide a fry-up every evening.'

Others, however, recall the Far East as a great improvement over the harsh desert conditions, one comment on Ceylon praising the 'lush green everywhere whilst the fresh fruit and vegetables provided us with Vitamin C we had lacked in the desert, soon banishing desert sores.' It was very much a case of local conditions being highly variable; for mobile squadrons - as most of the tactical units were - the situation was always uncertain, although in true RAF fashion most airmen were able to make the best of a bad situation and acquire almost anything that was not nailed down! Little of a culinary nature is recalled by RAF veterans of the desert and jungle war.

**The mobile canteen was a major part of RAF life, either at a bomber base in the UK or in the deserts of North Africa - a NAAFI wagon visits 112 Squadron's tent line, April 1942.**

RECIPES FROM THE FRONT LINE

# CHRISTMAS AT WAR

The RAF has always 'pushed the boat out' at Christmas even during the darkest days of the war. This No 4 FTS shot is undated but is probably pre-war late 1930s - the decoration and the general appearance of the tables looks pre-war.

'It will all be over by Christmas' has been the standard cry of politicians and Generals in every war since 1914 - and they have invariably been wrong. During the years of World War Two, five Christmas periods were spent 'at war', although by Christmas 1944 it was obvious to most that this would be the last. British military personnel did their best to mark the festive season regardless of where they were or how bad conditions were.

RAF operations were often curtailed during Christmas Day, although this very much depended on the prevailing military situation. Bomber Command for example flew 12 Hampden shipping reconnaissance sorties on December 25, 1939, but did not operate on Christmas Day 1940 or 1941. In the remaining war years, ops were confined to the night period December 24/25, the only large-scale effort being 1944

Compare this Christmas set-up with that for No 4 FTS. It looks much more austere - but nevertheless the effort was made each December 25 to lay on the full Christmas menu.

RECIPES FROM THE FRONT LINE

with over 200 Lancasters attacking various targets, plus a number of sorties by Mosquito and Halifax units.

In general, units were put on stand-by until mid morning but then stood down as soon as possible. This same principle applied to most units in the UK and overseas as commanders realised the importance of a 'normal' Christmas Day. It was still not possible, however, to release too many personnel to home leave. The major event of the day, especially in the overseas theatres, was Christmas dinner when the officers would act as waiters for the men, a tradition that continues at some stations to this day. It was also the Christmas dinner that has left its mark in the historical record with a selection of menu cards. Almost every unit, be it station or squadron, produced a menu for its festive meal and these prove to be excellent historical documents.

The detail on the menu depended upon the availability of an artist and his/her inclination to provide an interesting and informative piece of art. Most of the unit menu cards include the squadron badge and caricatures of aircraft, personnel and locations. These add up to a useful historical window. For example, the Christmas 1944 menu for 39 Squadron shows a Beaufighter departing top right and a Marauder arriving top left - most appropriate as this was the period when the squadron was saying goodbye to its Beaufighters and hello to its Marauders. The tent signifies the living accommodation at the squadron's base at Biferno, Italy (note the mountains in the background), whilst the officers, one sporting a handlebar moustache,

*'The major event of the day, especially in the overseas theatres, was Christmas dinner when the officers would act as waiters for the men, a tradition that continues at some stations to this day.'*

**Beer helped any Christmas party go well - the turkey may have been tough but the beer was still wet. One of the ideas was to get the 'other unit' drunk over dinner so that you could beat them in the afternoon games.**

arrive with dinner. I have no doubt that the cat also has some significance as does the airman tripping over.

# THE MENU
## STARTER

In terms of food featured on these wartime menus, tomato soup is the clear favourite in terms of a starter course, with this featuring on over 90 per cent of such menus regardless of the theatre of operations. A few other soups do feature from time to time, for example, crème of celery (RAF Harrow 1942), mock turtle (HQ 19 Group 1942) and even consommé Julienne (RAF Finningley 1940).

## MAIN COURSE

Roast turkey was almost invariably the main meat dish on offer, with the trimmings varying somewhat but often including the standard fare of sage and onion stuffing, potatoes, green peas and cauliflower - although the vegetable selection did show some variation, with Brussel sprouts appearing on numerous occasions. Roast pork with apple sauce also features, as a second meat, on the majority of menus and some also mention sausage, but without going into further details. The 1941 menu for the airmen's mess at RAF Luqa, Malta, includes the interesting statement that the menu might have been goat stew, pickled lizard, grilled ruff. Bread pudding - a reflection of the food shortages caused by the summer and autumn air assaults on the island.

## SWEET

Christmas pudding and brandy sauce leads the field in terms of popularity, although variations include rum sauce with the pudding; indeed, it is hard to find a menu that does not include Christmas pudding. This is usually followed by an offering of mince pies and fruit

The next major excuse for a good party came with VE Day (Victory Europe) and, as here, VJ Day (Victory Japan). Once again the tables featured serried ranks of beer bottles! No 212 Squadron repast at Redhills Lake.

RECIPES FROM THE FRONT LINE

**Smiling faces for what was often one of the best meals of the year.**

or nuts, although the latter two options are much more variable and some menus also include cheese and biscuits. With beer, minerals and coffee to wash it all down the RAF's Christmas menus were veritable feasts - at least on paper!

The part played by NAAFI in providing home comforts worldwide has never been truly recognised. The sight of the NAAFI wagon appearing outside of the hangar, or tent, was guaranteed to raise morale. It is often said that the super-strong NAAFI tea was a war-winning part of the British armed forces, certainly a great many airmen remember the distinctive taste, although the amounts of sugar some claim to have spooned in, when such a luxury was available, would no doubt have overpowered anything but the strongest of blends. Whilst tea was popular, it was the beer that made the Christmas meal go with a swing - the trick was to get the other team drunk and so hinder their efforts in the post-dinner competitions. The entertainment varied greatly from sporting events (particularly popular overseas where there was little opportunity for other types of leisure activity), through to unit plays and pantomimes, or even - for the really lucky ones - an ENSA concert. For all concerned it was a chance to get away from the war, if only for a day.

# WAAF MEMORIES

One member of the WAAF found her posting to RAF Chivenor in North Devon meant that she could no longer enjoy a spot of good Lancashire cooking - the dishes she most missed were Lancashire hot pot and Lancashire cheese and bacon pie.

## LANCASHIRE HOT POT

Take 1¹/₂lb of lamb chops and scrag (butcher will chop the meat) and roll in seasoned flour.
Warm a heavy casserole dish and put a tablespoon of dripping in the bottom.
Lay the meat in the dish.

Slice a large onion and place slices on top of the meat.
Slice two large potatoes into rounds and place on top of the onion.
Cut two or three more large potatoes into halves and put on top to form a crust.
Sprinkle top with a little flour and add stock/hot water to cover the sliced potatoes.
Put lid on and bake for 4 hours at 170°C or Gas 3.
Remove lid to allow top to brown.

## LANCASHIRE CHEESE AND BACON PIE

Chop 4oz of bacon into small pieces.
Finely chop one small onion and 4oz of Lancashire cheese.
Put in pan with a knob of butter and a little milk, bring to boil, stir and simmer for a few minutes.
Line buttered pie dish with shortcrust pastry.
Pour in cheese mix and sprinkle with grated cheese.
Bake in fairly hot oven (190°/Gas 5) for 15-20 minutes.

# CHAPTER FOUR
# RECIPES FROM THE FRONT LINE
# OF TODAY'S ROYAL AIR FORCE
# BY CAZ DYER

**The Officers' Mess, RAF Halton.**

# A YEAR IN THE LIFE...

The Royal Air Force has served and continues to serve on the front line. At a moment's notice it may be called upon to travel anywhere in the world, however remote for the service of Queen and country, whether it is a humanitarian, military or peacekeeping role.

At home or abroad, in the time-honoured tradition of the armed services, the Royal Air Force marks important dates in its calendar with special dinners and events. Some are yearly remembrances such as The Battle of Britain cocktail party, held on or around 15 September to raise a glass to 'The Few' who fought so bravely during the fight for Britain's skies at the beginning of World War Two. Others are special milestones, such as an anniversary to mark a squadron or station foundation, often celebrated with special dinners and beautifully designed cakes.

The Christmas and the summer balls, though, have to be the biggest social events of the RAF calendar, more informal than the dining-in nights but equally splendid.

The Mess and catering staff make these dinners and social occasions very special with a skill and professionalism second to none. As well as taking part in the inter-forces catering competitions, the catering wing also helps to nurture young talent and gives up its time to help with children's events.

The following chapter gives you just a taste of what the Royal Air Force achieves on the catering front line from Burns' Night at RAF Leuchars to an Oktoberfest at RAF Brüggen.

# BURNS' NIGHT AT RAF LEUCHARS

A Burns' Night supper is held each year on 25 January to mark the birthday of Robert Burns, Scotland's national poet. Although wearing a kilt is not compulsory, it is an appropriate touch; the ladies may wear a tartan sash.

The meal begins with the grace *(opposite)* and ceremoniously the haggis is held aloft by the head chef, while being piped into the dining room to the delight of the invited guests. After the completion of the meal, the diners rise to toast The Queen with a dram of whisky followed by the immortal memory to the dead poet. A dram of whisky is essential for the toasts and is usually served throughout the meal. Post-supper entertainment may include a guest orator who will give a recitation of some of the great poet's work.

What follows is a typical menu for a Burns' Night supper.

*The Selkirk Grace*
*Some hae meat, and canna eat,*
*And some wad eat, that want it;*
*But we hae meal and we can eat,*
*And sae the Lord be thank it.*
**Robert Burns (1759-1796)**

## COCK A LEEKIE SOUP
## SERVES 4-6 PERSONS

*'After the completion of the meal, the diners rise to toast The Queen with a dram of whisky followed by the immortal memory to the dead poet.'*

A 2¹/₂lb-3lb chicken is placed with its giblets and an onion in a large saucepan. Water is added and then brought to the boil. The pan is then covered and left to simmer for 1¹/₂ hours, any scum being skimmed off as it boils.

Once the chicken is tender, the meat is stripped from the carcass, the giblets and bones were discarded and the stock strained, then the meat is added back to the stock. 6 leeks are cut into long thin strips, another onion chopped and one small carrot grated. These along with 2oz of long grain rice are added to the stock, which is then brought back to the boil, covered and simmered for a further 30 minutes. It is finally seasoned with salt and pepper to taste and garnished with chopped parsley to serve.

### MENU

Cock a leekie soup
(A light clear soup of chicken, leeks and onion)

Haggis, tatties and neeps
(Traditional haggis served with mashed potatoes and creamed carrots and swede)

## ATHOLE BROSE
## SERVES 4-6 PERSONS

Roast sirloin of Aberdeen Angus
Roasted potatoes with wild garlic
Roasted carrots and parsnips with heather honey
Calabrise florets

2oz of medium oatmeal are toasted until golden brown and then left to cool. One pint of double cream is beaten until thick. The cooled oatmeal and 4 level tablespoons of clear honey are stirred into the cream, and 4 tablespoons of whisky are mixed in just before serving.

Athole brose
(Toasted oatmeal laced with honey and whisky)

The dessert is served in small glasses, garnished with some reserved toasted oatmeal and drizzled with a little honey.

Coffee with home-made Highland shortbread

MENU PREPARED BY CPL A P ARMSTRONG, OFFICERS' MESS RAF LEUCHARS.

# THE ROYAL VISIT TO RAF MARHAM

Royal Air Force Marham will become the largest front-line station in Great Britain with the return of the last RAF squadrons from Germany.

The Officers' Mess has an excellent reputation for producing a high standard of cuisine and has entertained many important visitors throughout the years. The Station's Honorary Air Commodore, Her Majesty The Queen, took luncheon in the Officers' Mess during a recent visit.

While the salon orchestra of the Royal Air Force provided the music, the invited guests enjoyed fillet saddle of lamb.

The Mess chef who prepared the dishes has given permission to print his recipes; they would make an excellent dinner party menu.

## BREAST OF TURKEY, SPINACH AND PARMESAN ROULADE

Slices of fresh turkey breast are placed on a square of cling film, seasoned, and a thin coating of whole grain mustard is spread over them. Trimmed spinach leaves are then placed on top of the turkey breasts, followed by skinned and roasted red pepper slices and Parmesan cheese. The turkey breasts are rolled and steam baked for 40 minutes, then sliced on the angle. The remainder forms a tower and the slices are fanned around the plate. This is served with a cream horseradish sauce, which is lightly whipped cream with horseradish folded in to taste.

It makes a stunning and effective contrast that is both tasty and satisfying.

Her Majesty The Queen being introduced to the Officers' Mess manager and staff before taking luncheon in the Officers' Mess, RAF Marham.

Final inspection of the table, dressed with the Mess silver and beautiful flower decorations.

# FILLET SADDLE OF LAMB

One of the tenderest pieces of the lamb is the 'eye' that runs through the loin, forming part of the saddle. For such an important occasion and to obtain consistency, the chef decided to purchase whole saddles, and butcher them himself. Once the saddles are trimmed of all sinew, a cut is made through the centre so they can be stuffed with a lamb fillet wrapped in leek. The leek is cut in half lengthways, rinsed and blanched for two minutes. Once the fillet has been frozen it is wrapped with a piece of leek. Freezing the fillet allows the leek to stick to the meat. While still frozen, the fillet is pushed through the cut made in the 'eye', then lightly seasoned, sealed in a frying pan on a high heat then roasted for 15 minutes in a hot oven, gas 6 or 200°C. It is then left to rest before carving. The meat is lovely and pink, which contrasts against the leek. It is mouth-watering, tender and especially tasty! The crispy vegetables are an assortment of root vegetables, parsnip, swede, celeriac, potato and carrot, simply coated in besan flour (available from Oriental outlets), dusted off in a sieve then deep fried until golden.

# TRIO OF PARFAIT

Puréed fruit is added to a basic parfait recipe, which is coconut cream, mango and strawberry. Each one is made in a different shape but built together as a whole. The bottom consists of the mango parfait frozen in a triangular mould, and then sliced. Sitting on top of the mango is the coconut parfait, which is put into a round mould but frozen at a slant for effect. Topping them is the strawberry parfait frozen in a round disc. All three are assembled together and a chocolate RAF crest is placed on the strawberry parfait. Serve with a fresh fruit and lime sauce.

# CHILDREN'S EASTER
# HOLIDAY FUN

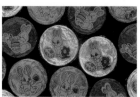

The children of RAF personnel like to do the odd bit of cooking too. At holiday times, it is always difficult to keep your offspring occupied, but organised holiday activities help to make the time go by much more quickly for children, and the parents!

The cookery demonstration classes are always over subscribed and the catering wing always puts on a fine show. But cooking for kids is only really fun when you can get your hands in and get mucky.

At a children's cookery class at RAF Marham, Cpl Julie Whitfield was helping the kids to make chocolate biscuits decorated with icing. The best bit, the children agreed, was icing faces on to the biscuits, using as many lurid colours as possible. Despite this, the biscuits taste thoroughly delicious.

The children had also decorated cake boxes to carry their goodies home. Some were decorated with flower motifs, others had 'keep out' written on them. As well as the chocolate cookies inside the cake boxes, there were gingerbread men and chocolate cornflake nests with miniature eggs .

So, if it's raining outside, why don't you get out the mixing bowl and have some fun making biscuits with the kids. Your kitchen floor will never look the same again!

The recipe, which follows, is enough to feed a small army, just alter the quantities in proportion to the required amount.

# CHOCOLATE HEAVEN COOKIES

Cream together the caster sugar and margarine until fluffy.

Sift in flour, cocoa powder and baking powder. Add in vanilla, beat until combined.

Take a small piece, the size of a walnut, and roll into a ball. Place the ball onto a pre-greased baking tray (the mixture will flatten to biscuit shape during cooking). Repeat until all mixture used.

Bake in a pre-heated oven, 180°C for 10 minutes.

Decorate once cooled with piped icing or to make it even more chocolatey, melted chocolate.

2lb caster sugar
2lb margarine
2lb plain flour
1/2 lb cocoa powder
2oz baking powder
2 drops of vanilla essence

# MARS BAR CRISPIES

This recipe is from Malaika Goldsmith, aged three, and it's just perfect for Easter as well.

Melt the Mars Bar in a large saucepan over a low heat.

Remove from heat and mix in the crispies.

Place in paper cases and put in fridge to set.

Decorate with small sugar-coated chocolate eggs.

3 Mars Bars chopped into pieces
2oz margarine
3 cups of Rice Crispies

# A SUMMER MENU FROM RAF LOSSIEMOUTH

Located on the Moray Firth coast in the north of Scotland, RAF Lossiemouth is the largest Tornado base and busiest operational airfield in the RAF at present. It's fine but cold weather and excellent flying areas make it one of the best locations in the UK for flying training, and it is home to two operational Squadrons, 12 and 617, and the Tornado Operational Conversion Unit (OCU), XV(R) Squadron.

The head chef at RAF Lossiemouth devised the following recipes for the Station Commander for a dinner party at The Old Manse (the Station Commander's residence) during the summer. It is a delightfully refreshing menu using some wonderful local ingredients.

## SPEYSIDE OAK SMOKED WHISKY SALMON WITH CREAM AND HERB SAUCE

**SERVES 4**

4 x 6oz Speyside marinated smoked salmon fillet per person that can be purchased from the Higher Scottish Regions. Poach in hot fish stock for 8 minutes.

Sauce:
2 shallots
1 teaspoon of chopped parsley
teaspoon of mixed chervil and tarragon
2oz butter
1 teaspoon of flour
1 teaspoon of Dijon mustard
10 floz double cream
2 egg yolks
a touch of lemon
season salt/pepper

The tumbling waters of Speyside provides the king of fish - the salmon. Locally marinated until rich and tender then smoked with the oak chips from the casks of Speyside's most distinguished distiller of malt whisky ('Macallan').

Cook the shallots and herbs in the butter until softened. Add the flour, then dilute the cream and add mustard lemon juice, seasoning and cook for ten minutes. Finally whisk in the egg yolks and then your sauce is ready to serve.

# Roasted Root Vegetables with Rhubarb

A selection of root vegetables blended with the delicate taste of rhubarb.

Cut all the vegetables into small batons and blanche all vegetables except rhubarb in hot salted water for 3 minutes. Pan fry all vegetables including rhubarb in a small amount of olive oil and then place in a medium oven for 15 minutes.

**SERVES 4**

4oz carrot

4oz rhubarb

4oz parsnip

4oz baby purple turnip

# Rothes Glen Potato Cake with Oatmeal

Potato cake blended with chestnuts and coated in oatmeal.

Peel and boil potatoes until soft. Shape into a round potato cake and coat with oatmeal. Drain well and mix in egg yolk, chestnuts, butter and season. Pan fry on the top of the hob in hot oil and cook both sides to a golden brown and then serve.

**SERVES 4**

Potato cake blended with chestnuts and coated in oatmeal.

1lb potatoes

1 egg yolk

1oz butter

1oz chestnut

season salt/pepper

# THE ANNIVERSARY OF RAF LYNEHAM

**WO Dave Dunk pictured with the 60th Anniversary cake he created.**

On Saturday 18 May 1940, RAF Lyneham, Wiltshire, opened for business as an Aircraft Storage Unit, complete with four officers, one other rank and 15 civilians - but no aircraft. Since those humble beginnings the station has become the RAF's only tactical support base, flying thousands of hours and millions of miles.

From Liberators and Dakotas in World War Two, through Yorks, Hastings and Comets to the Hercules, which have been based there for 33 years, the personnel and aircraft have been at the forefront of both military and relief operations. These have included the evacuation of wounded troops from the continent during World War Two; the Berlin Airlift; the Suez Crisis; famine in Africa; the Falklands to the Balkans and now Sierra Leone.

So to honour those past and present, and, in the finest tradition, RAF Lyneham celebrated its Diamond Jubilee on 18 May 2000. Her Royal Highness the Princess Royal, RAF Lyneham's Honorary Air Commodore attended a dinner to celebrate this special occasion.

To mark the occasion, Warrant Officer Catering, Dave Dunk, created a magnificent cake, which featured many of the station's past aircraft, badges of the various units and, at the top, the RAF Eagle.

The 25lb cake was crafted with such skill, involved many hours of work and demonstrated the professionalism of the catering wing. The cake didn't just look fantastic, it tasted good too, and was cut up and donated to local old people's homes.

# The summer ball, RAF Halton

Throughout June and July, summer balls are held at RAF bases across the country and abroad. These are probably the biggest social occasions in the Service's calendar.

The event is often themed and the rooms are decorated by different units on station, all vying for the prize of the best-dressed room.

An 'around the world' theme is always very popular, from the Orient to the Americas, enabling the Mess chefs to create many international dishes. Delicate Thai curries are served in the main dining-room next to the colonial buffet and outside on the patio the smoky atmosphere of the barbecue entices you with beefsteaks and ribs.

The entertainment can vary from fairground dodgems, roving magicians to live bands. If you are still hungry and awake, there is always the survivors' breakfast, which is served between four and five in the morning.

RAF Halton is a magnificent setting for a summer ball. Halton House has served as the Officers' Mess from 1918, but previously it was one of the five Rothschild mansions, gracing the Buckinghamshire countryside. It was built between 1881-1883 in a spectacular French style.

RAF Halton invited a Thai chef to prepare and cook the oriental food at their summer ball and Chalaem Davies donated the recipe, which follows;

**RAF Halton's Officers' Mess.**

## Chicken Panang

Heat 3½ tablespoons of oil.

Add the curry paste, cook until the paste begins to soften.

Add the coconut milk and the chicken.

Slice the lime leaves very finely and add to the chicken.

Add the chicken stock and simmer gently for 30 minutes.

Serve with a portion of jasmine rice.

2 tablespoons Thai red curry paste

3 lime leaves

400ml of coconut milk

3 tablespoons oyster sauce

1 teaspoon sugar

3lb cooked chicken breast

oil for cooking

½ pint of chicken stock

pinch of salt

# THE BATTLE OF BRITAIN, RAF COLTISHALL

## BY SQN LDR ED BULPETT

*'Battle of Britain day is celebrated on 15 September, marking the height of the battle.'*

The construction of Royal Air Force Coltishall began in February 1939, but it was pressed into use as a fighter station in May 1940 while still incomplete. The first squadron to operate from the station was No 66 flying Spitfires, and it was joined in June 1940 by No 242 Squadron, flying Hurricanes. The latter squadron had returned from France to refit and was placed under the command of Sqn Ldr Douglas Bader.

Coltishall was in No 12 Group during the Battle of Britain and a pilot of No 66 Squadron destroyed the first enemy aircraft in the battle, a Dornier 17, in the early hours of 10 July 1940. As the battle progressed the station was used as a base for resting squadrons from No 11 Group in south east England, but the station's own squadrons played an aggressive part, belonging to the celebrated 'Duxford Wing' and destroying a total of 80 aircraft. The station was attacked several times and a number of people were killed, although on one occasion ground defenders succeeded in destroying a Heinkel 111 with Lewis guns. Such famous 'aces' as Stamford Tuck, 'Sailor' Malan and Johnnie Johnson all flew from the base during World War Two.

Moving to the present day, Royal Air Force Coltishall is now the base for three Jaguar squadrons, Nos 6, 41(F) and 54(F). The roles of the Jaguar are as fighter-bomber attack and tactical reconnaissance infra red (TRI) and are assigned to NATO as part of the Rapid Reaction Force. The station commemorated its sixtieth anniversary on 1 July 2000.

Battle of Britain day is celebrated on 15 September, marking the height of the battle. Across the Royal Air Force it is a day of remembrance to 'The Few', who protected our skies during those dark days. Cocktail parties are held on or around this date and we raise a glass to them all.

RECIPES FROM THE FRONT LINE

# 'A PILOT'S RETURN'

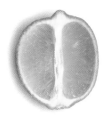

Put the ice in a shaker.
Add all the ingredients and shake until cold.
Strain into a Paris goblet.
Serve with a slice of orange and one ice cube.

This is a refreshing drink with a warm pink colour; the quantities are for two servings - so ladies why not treat a friend! (The Cassis may be substituted with Grenadine)

FROM CPL MICHAEL J BROOM,
OFFICERS' MESS, RAF COLTISHALL.

25ml Vodka

25ml Cointreau

5ml Cassis

200ml orange juice

small dash of lime

2 drops of Angostura Bitters

add bitter lemon to taste

5 ice cubes

# ALL AROUND THE WORLD

## BY FLT LT HOUSELY, TORNADO GR4 PILOT

Over the last ten years the Royal Air Force has kindly flown me to a whole host of locations around Europe, North America and the Middle East. Occasional trips to more unusual destinations, such as Malaysia and Chile, do emerge, but you need to be on the right squadron at the right time. However, in the fast jet world these exotic locations are now rarely visited due to time or money. The journeys abroad vary from a quick stay over a few days, to an exercise lasting a couple of weeks or a complete squadron deployment lasting 2½ months. The armed forces are renowned for marching on their stomachs, and without a doubt food has played a major part in our enjoyment or morale when away from home. Food can completely change one's opinion of a good or bad detachment.

On two such detachments a Mobile Catering Unit had been tasked with feeding the hungry troops. On both occasions they surprised us

*'Here the Italian chef tried to produce food for the discerning British palate. It rarely tasted of the fresh herbs one might expect and was guaranteed to be offered with chips.'*

with the quality of the food on offer. At the Prince Sultan Air Base, in the middle of the Saudi Arabian desert, the staff produced a 'taste of home' with the aid of migrant workers.

They came to a great compromise as to the duties within the kitchen. In return for authentic curry recipes, the migrant workers were taught pastry and pudding making skills. As far as we were concerned this was a fine arrangement and meant we survived on curries for nearly the whole month-long detachment. In sub-zero conditions in Norway, they produced roasts, pasta and pies, all with a full complement of sauces and vegetables, followed by puddings like your mother used to make.

Stationed at Bodo, on a headland out into the North Sea, a number of engineers elected to fish while the aircrew completed their missions to the north around Bardufoss. Fish, therefore, formed a major part of our diet over the two week detachment. The flavour-filled 'just caught' taste of our fresh fish was hard to beat.

Heading south to Denmark during a visit to Copenhagen gave me the chance to try fish prepared in a completely different way. I felt it was time to try something new, although raw fish does not sit high on my list of 'must try this' style dishes. Rather than completely raw, the herring had been warmed, but not cooked, and was served with a caper vinaigrette. I was pleasantly surprised, and would heartily recommend one of their traditional dishes.

Over the years a favourite RAF destination has been Italy, both for training and as a staging post into the Balkans. For the training aspect, this is mainly due to the good weather factor. My journeys to Italy have been a mixture of business and pleasure, but in every instance, apart from the flying, it is the food that has made the greatest impression. One black spot was the dinner at RAF Decimomannu. Here the Italian chef tried to produce food for the discerning British palate. It rarely tasted of the fresh herbs one might expect and was guaranteed to be offered with chips.

Away from the base we sampled perfect pasta in Cagliari and thin crispy pizza with minimal, but flavour-packed, toppings that do beg the question as to why the deep pan pizza was ever invented. On one evening we accepted an invitation to a restaurant run by the family of one of the base's kitchen staff. A luminous welcome drink was followed by wine from the family vineyard, finishing with grappa that could be used to strip paint. The courses arrived at such a rate we soon ran out of table space. before roast pig arrived, people were reluctant to allow antipasto and pasta dishes to be cleared away before they had the chance to sample everything.

The theme of great choice was also evident when on a squadron exchange with 106 Gruppo, a Tornado GR1 Squadron based at Ghedi near Lake Garda. Rather than grabbing a quick sandwich, the squadron retires daily to the officers' mess for lunch. They believe in a 'light working lunch', yet even after three courses you do not feel bloated, as each course complements the next. Halfway through our stay we were treated to a meal in a restaurant well off the beaten track, one in which you need to speak the language or have your own translator and, like Norfolk, to know where you are going before you set off.

In recent months I have been fortunate enough to have twice visited the USA on squadron deployments, once to the bright lights of Las Vegas, and more recently Salt Lake City. On both occasions the intention was to practice operational low flying down to 100 feet, and to drop a variety of 1000lb bombs. As far as aircrew are concerned, this amounts to some of the best peacetime flying available anywhere in the world. The USA certainly provides a huge variety of terrain and flying challenges, but can the same be said of the food?

Eating out in the States differs markedly to back home in the UK - that is, of course, unless in an American restaurant chain. The enormous choice of places to dine should surely lead to a wonderful selection of cuisine from around the globe. Decisions as to the style of your evening meal have to be made. Fear not! All is not as it seems! Wherever you choose, all that will actually differ on the menu will be the company logo. All will offer steaks, burgers, chicken, Tex Mex, pasta and salads. The 'healthy option' of the salad is accompanied with a wicked dip or dressing: ranch; Italian (they would cringe), blue cheese; honey and mustard; thousand island, etc! Service comes with a smile (and a well-rehearsed script). Communication may prove to be a problem as it becomes so apparent that we are two nations separated by a common language. Only the question or script is important, not the answer. 'How are you this evening?' does not appear to require an answer. Rather than disturb the waiter/waitress' flow, my advice is to 'stick with the programme' and accept that the monologue must be followed to ensure you receive the meal of you choice. You can try avoiding the script altogether by completing your selection of soup, salad, dressing, main course, type of potatoes/veg etc without pausing for breath. The meals are well presented and portions generous, but since the restaurant chains' policy is rigidly adhered to, the food is unlikely to be a gastronomic assault on your taste buds. After a few days you start to crave 'undressed' salad or a dish spiced with something other than chilli. It becomes apparent how sanitised their food has become. It's at this point that one realises how fortunate we are here in the UK, especially in Norfolk, where independent restaurants and pubs still survive in abundance and have menus that change depending upon the season and the availability of produce.

*'After a few days you start to crave 'undressed' salad or a dish spiced with something other than chilli. It becomes apparent how sanitised their food has become.'*

In Kuwait, the American influence is clear to see. To avoid a lengthy decision process when choosing a meal, they simplify the menu. This is done by removing everything other than chicken and rice from the menu and changing its name on a regular basis.

For the most outrageously bland food we visited Goose Bay, Canada. Here we used to be fed by Can Cat (Canada Catering). Sadly, the food often lived up to its abbreviated name. They were able to produce ham or turkey sandwiches that differed only by colour. Fortunately for us, the remainder of the packed lunches were easily identified brand items.

In recent years the Tornado GR1 fleet has been on Operation Northern Watch. This involved patrolling the skies over Northern Iraq alongside the Americans and the French. We were stationed at Incirlik Air Base near the city of Adana, Turkey. Although the Americans had kindly ensured we had burger bars and the like on station, most people elected to eat in the large number of local restaurants on the 'strip' just outside the main gate.

You would always receive a warm welcome and, almost without asking, once seated food would start to arrive. Flat bread, similar to naan breads except up to five feet long, was placed down the centre of the table. It would either be plain or topped with cheese and/or chilli. This was accompanied by warm humus or spiced soft cheese. It is in these few restaurants that they serve the finest fried calamari I have tasted. It is cooked in a crisp batter and comes with simple lemon juice and garlic dip. Since it was fresh and cooked rapidly, it was not in the slightest bit rubbery. For the main course, kebabs naturally feature heavily on the menu, although more often than not the tava dishes were more popular. The tava consisted of meat, fresh tomatoes and herbs, garlic, mushrooms and chilli to taste. These are cooked as portions in terracotta dishes, in a clay oven. Although hygiene did not appear to be top of the owner's list of worries, I don't remember people falling ill from eating this freshly prepared food, unlike eating at the burger bar.

*'It is in these few restaurants that they serve the finest fried calamari I have tasted.'*

Overall the Royal Air Force has allowed me to visit a number of places I might not have otherwise considered as a civilian. Unfortunately, due to the nature of the job, we may have shied away from the true character that these places have to offer. We have never really had to mix with the locals and as far as I can remember, it is only in Italy and Turkey where a local has shown us the way. In both instances I have been unable to find an equivalent here in the UK.

**Bavarian themed menu**

Bean and Tomato Soup

Sauerkraut with Pork
Mac Sausage
Sausage and Chutney Flan

Stuffed Peppers
Roasted Vegetables and Bean Salad
Bavarian Rice Medley
München Potatoes
Blue Cheese, Pear and Walnut
Salad

Apfel Torten
German Baked Cheesecake
Apple and Cider Spiced Cake

# OKTOBERFEST FROM RAF BRÜGGEN

The traditional Oktoberfest is held in Munich, Bavaria, in late September/October each year. Originally and by tradition only the eight breweries of the city of Munich are allowed to erect marquees depicting their brewery on the festival fairground.

Each marquee will have a different theme, and provide differing types of German food. The marquee can hold up to 5,000 people each, and German Oompah Bands and other live entertainment. The foods served can be anything from spit roasted oxen and chickens to a variety of German sausages (wurst). German salads and pretzels, schnitzels, roast kassler and of course the original sauerkraut are served throughout the day, from midday to midnight.

Many RAF Stations have an Oktoberfest or Bavarian themed evening. The following menu (opposite) and selected recipes are from RAF Brüggen, Germany.

# SAUERKRAUT WITH PORK

Grease a large casserole with lard or dripping and pile in half the cabbage. Add the carrots, onions and bouquet garni. Cover with remaining cabbage.

Top with the ham knuckle, glass of wine and ham bouillon. Season. Cover, bring to the boil and simmer or casserole for 1 hour.

Add the belly of pork, cover and cook for a further 1½ hours.

Then remove the pork and add the potatoes and sausages and cook for a further 30 minutes.

Remove the bouquet garni and cloves and return the pork belly for 10 minutes to reheat.

Arrange the sauerkraut in a large dish garnished with potatoes, sausages and sliced meat.

**SERVES 10**

4 ¼lb (2kg) white cabbage, shredded

3 carrots, diced

2 onions peeled and studded with a clove

bouquet garni

1 uncooked ham knuckle

1 glass of Hock

1¾ pints (1 litre) ham bouillon

seasoning

1½ - 2lb (675-900g) belly of pork

2½ lb (1.1kg) potatoes

6-8 pork sausages

# GERMAN BAKED CHEESECAKE

Grease and line the base of a 20½ cm (8") square cake tin. Combine the biscuits, melted butter and nutmeg, use to line the base of the tin.

Blend the cheese, caster sugar and lemon rind, fold in egg yolks and soured cream.

Whisk the egg whites until stiff and fold into the cheese mixture.

Sprinkle the mixed peel and raisins on to the biscuit base and cover with the cream cheese mixture.

Bake at 140°C (275°F) Mark 1 for 1 hour or until the mixture is set. Leave to cool in the tin. Cut into 9 squares. Serve dusted with icing sugar

6oz (175g) digestive biscuits, crushed

3oz (75g) butter melted

½ teaspoon ground nutmeg

12oz (350g) cream cheese

3oz (75g) caster sugar

grated rind of 2 lemons

4 eggs separated

7½ floz (215ml) soured cream

2oz (50g) mixed peel

30z (75g) seedless raisins

icing sugar to dust

CONGHAM HALL HERB GARDEN

# Chapter Five
# Recipes from the front line
# of commerce and leading
# Norfolk restaurants

Front line industries associated with RAF Marham and leading Norfolk restaurants have kindly provided recipes using the best of Norfolk's produce. Enjoy!

# ANGLIAN WATER'S
## PERFECT CUP OF TEA

fresh cold tap water

kettle

tea (loose or bagged 1 heaped
teaspoon per cup)

teapot (preferably with spout at
bottom)

strainer

milk (full cream produces more
scum than semi-skimmed)

sugar (optional)

bone china cup(s)

Empty kettle of all old water (plants love it!) and refill from the cold water tap. Bring to a full boil. In the meantime place hot water from the tap into the teapot to warm.

Place loose or bagged tea into the warmed teapot, cover with freshly boiled water and let stand for 3 minutes.

Carefully rotate teapot around 3 times to encourage circulation of water through tea.

Add room temperature milk into cup and pour contents of the teapot through a strainer thus avoiding encouragement of surface scum. Add sugar to taste and sit down with biscuits or other refreshment of your choice.

# BERNARD MATTHEWS'
## TURKEY FILLETS WITH MUSHROOM SAUCE

**SERVES 4**

4 turkey fillets

500g mushrooms -
sliced

200g creme fraiche

salt and pepper

Fry mushrooms until golden brown. Remove from pan, and then fry turkey fillets with a little salt and pepper until lightly browned.

Return mushrooms to the pan, then add creme fraiche and simmer gently until turkey fillets are cooked and sauce slightly reduced.

Serve with either new potatoes or rice, and fresh seasonal vegetables.

# CAMPBELL'S
## TUNA PASTA BAKE

### SERVES 4

7oz (200g) pasta shapes

295g can Campbell's Condensed Cream of Sweetcorn or Mushroom Soup

7fl oz (200ml) milk

1/2 bunch spring onions, chopped

200g can tuna, drained

3½ oz (100g) Cheddar, grated

Cook pasta as pack instructs. Drain. Stir in soup, milk, onions and tuna and heat through, stirring regularly.

Transfer to 1.2 litre flame-proof dish, top with cheese and grill until golden. (Or bake for 30 minutes in hot oven.)

# COLMAN'S
## KIDNEYS A LA GOURMET

This is a recipe taken from the Mustard Club Recipe Book circa 1926.

Procure by fair means, or foul, a potato of aldermanic proportions; one about eight inches long, five inches broad, and three inches deep: in short an exceedingly well nourished spud.

Now take two sheep's kidneys, split them and skin them. Rub a little dry mustard, pepper and salt into the cut sides.

Cut your potato lengthways into two exact halves, do not peel, then with a tablespoon hoick out two recesses in each half big enough to place a kidney in (try to imagine a jewel in its velvet case).

Pepper a small rasher of streaky bacon both sides, place the top of the kidneys reposing in one half of the potato, then taking the other half complete with kidney halved, place the two closely together and with an exact fit. Tie tightly with a piece of raffia and bake in a hot oven until done.

Cooked in the embers of a camp fire this is a dish fit for the gods.

Kidneys and mustard came into the world together.

RECIPES FROM THE FRONT LINE

# EASTERN ENERGY

*'John Eley, otherwise known as the Cooking Canon, shares the secret of combining hearty meals with energy efficient cooking on behalf of Eastern Energy.*

*A great dish for the children, either as a high-energy teatime treat during the school holidays, a warming breakfast before school or a simple pudding at any time.'*

## BANANAS IN PYJAMAS

The filling:
1 banana per person
icing sugar
maple syrup

The batter:
4oz plain flour
1/2 teaspoon salt
1 x 1.5ml spoon cooking oil
125 ml milk
2 egg whites

Calories:
126 per fritter, including a teaspoon of maple syrup

Sift the flour and salt together. Make a well in the middle and add the oil and milk (already mixed together). Stir to make a batter.

Whisk the egg whites and fold them gently into the mixture. Cut the peeled bananas in half lengthways, then half again. Dip them in the batter and deep fry until crisp and golden.

Remove from oil with a slotted spoon and drain on kitchen towel to absorb the excess oil. Sprinkle with icing sugar and serve with the maple syrup. Mind those sticky fingers!

# THE HABERDASHERS' COMPANY
## BANANA BREAD

Grease and line the base and ends of a 2lb loaf tin. Heat the oven to 180°C/350°F or Gas mark 4.

Sift the flour and salt into a large mixing bowl. Add the butter, cut into pieces, and rub into the dry ingredients, until the mixture is similar to breadcrumbs.

Rinse the glace cherries under warm water to remove the sugar coating, then pat dry and cut into quarters. Add the sugar, sultanas or seedless raisins, the walnuts and glace cherries. Mix together and hollow out the centre of the ingredients. Crack the eggs into the hollow.

Peel and mash the bananas in a separate bowl and then add to the eggs. Using a wooden spoon beat all the ingredients thoroughly to a soft consistency.

Pour the mixture into the tin and spread evenly.

Place in the centre of the oven and bake for 1½ hours.
Cool before removing from the tin.

The bread is best eaten a day or two after making, with or without butter.

8oz (225g) self-raising flour

½ level teaspoon salt

4oz (100g) butter

6oz (175g) caster sugar

4oz (100g) sultanas or seedless raisins

1oz (25g) chopped walnuts

4oz (100g) glace cherries

2 large eggs

1lb (450g) ripe bananas and another banana

# ROCOCO

## ROCOCO'S
## PUFF PASTRY OF CROMER
## CRAB AND NORFOLK BROWN
## SHRIMPS WITH HERB BEURRE BLANC

**Nick Anderson, Chef patron of Rococo.**

**SERVES 4**

4 medium dressed crabs
puff pastry
250ml fish stock
50ml Noilly Pratt
10g chopped shallots
25ml double cream
150g brown peeled shrimps
unsalted butter (cut into cubes)
fresh herbs (chives, chervil, basil)
fresh lemon juice
10g finely chopped red pepper

Cut puff pastry into 10cm rounds and bake.
Separate the white and brown crabmeat, retain brown for another use.

Warm the white meat in a moderate oven (covered with foil) with a little butter and seasoning until warm.

Place together in a saucepan the fish stock, shallots, Noilly Pratt and bring to boil. Reduce this by 2/3 add cream and simmer for 2 mins.

Whilst still on the heat add cubes of butter one at a time stirring each one in until sauce thickens.

Add in shrimps, red pepper and chopped herbs and adjust seasoning. Add a few drops of lemon juice.

### TO SERVE
On four plates place the bottom half of the puff pastry, top this with the white crabmeat.

Spoon a little of the sauce over the crab and put the top on.
Spoon the remaining sauce around the plates.

RECIPES FROM THE FRONT LINE

# FISHES'
## BRANCASTER MUSSELS
## AND OYSTERS BAKED WITH GARLIC

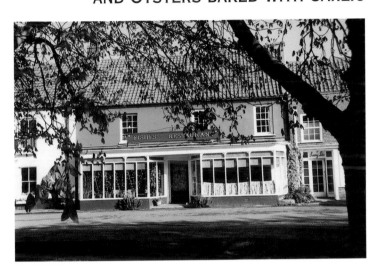

Open oysters - watch no shell with meat - leave in deeper shell with liquid.

Steam mussels in large pan, (with a well fitting lid), in small quantity of dry white wine. Strong heat, shake once or twice for 4 minutes. Check all should be open. Drain and cool slightly. Separate, leaving mussels in $^{1}/_{2}$ shell.

Arrange on 1 (or 4 ) ovenproof plates and dot with garlic butter (melted if easier).

Sprinkle with buttery crumbs

Put in hot oven until lightly browned for 10 minutes. Garnish with lemon (lots!)

Eat with good bread and butter, and dry white wine.

**FOR 4 (INCREASE/DECREASE TO MATCH HUNGER)**

12 oysters
4 pints mussels
buy on coast direct from fishermen

For garlic butter:
200g unsalted butter softened
1 tablespoon chopped parsley
1 tablespoon chopped spring onion
3 good cloves garlic pressed
black pepper
All above thoroughly mixed
Soft breadcrumbs moistened with a little melted garlic butter

# CONGHAM HALL'S
## HOME GROWN BRAMLEY APPLE AND ALMOND TART WITH BLACKCURRANT MINT CHANTILLY CREAM

250g sweet pastry
4 large Bramley apples
300g frangipane
50g flaked almond
100g sugar

Line and half bake a 10-inch tart ring.

Peel and quarter the apples and poach in water and sugar until tender. Pour the frangipane mixture into the half-baked tart ring.

Drain the apples and place on top of the frangipane.
Bake for 30-40 minutes at 180°C until cooked.

For the Frangipane:
60g butter
60g sugar
3 eggs
60g almonds
40g self raising flour

### FOR THE FRANGIPANE
Make the frangipane by whipping the butter and sugar, add the eggs, then the dry ingredients.

For the Chantilly Cream:
250ml double cream
100g icing sugar
4 drops vanilla essence
1 vanilla pod
25g blackcurrant mint

### FOR THE CHANTILLY CREAM
Mix the cream, icing sugar and vanilla until whipped, serve with the hot tart.

# THE LIFEBOAT INN'S
## MUSSELS

*The Lifeboat Inn*

16th Century Smugglers Ale House

Sweat off shallots and garlic in a shallow saucepan with lid on. Add mussels and stir for 1 minute, put the lid on and steam for a further 2 minutes. Add white wine and reduce by half.

Add cream and reduce by half.
Finish with freshly ground pepper and parsley.

Serve with crusty bread and butter.

Owen Colville (Head Chef)

1 small knob of butter

1 large shallot finely diced

1 clove of crushed garlic

400ml cream

250ml white wine

16 Brancaster mussels

freshly ground black pepper

chopped parsley

**MORSTON HALL**
Restaurant and Accommodation

# MORSTON HALL'S
## CLASSIC LEMON TART

7 eggs

rind of two lemons and juice of four

10oz (250g) caster sugar

6 fl oz (170ml) double cream

1 egg yolk (for sealing the pastry base)

*'Keeping on the theme of updated classics, a really good lemon tart just has to sit proudly on the top of the pile for me. The end result of this lemon tart is a wonderful smooth, deep, intensely flavoured lemon filling surrounded by crisp, sweet pastry and really the only accompaniment in my opinion would be a blob of mascapone.'* (Galton Blackiston, Head Chef and owner).

Line a 10 inch (25cm) pastry base with sweet pastry, cover with foil and baking beans. Bake blind in a moderate oven gas mark 4 or 350°F until pastry has firmed and is just about fully cooked.

Whilst the pastry is cooking make the filling. Whisk the eggs and sugar together in a bowl then add the lemon juice and rind, finally stir in the double cream.

When the pastry base has browned around the edges, remove from the oven and take out the baking beans. Now while the tart base is still warm, brush liberally with egg yolk especially in any cracks which may have appeared around the edges.

Then place back in the oven to allow the egg yolk to seal the base and sides. If not convinced that the tart base is sufficiently sealed well, do it again.

Now turn the oven down to gas mark 2 or 250°F and pour the mixture into the still hot pastry case and cook in the oven for about 40 minutes until just set.

Then remove from the oven and allow to cool before serving with a good dusting of icing sugar.

RECIPES FROM THE FRONT LINE

# LYNFORD HALL'S
## ORGANIC PECAN PIE

LYNFORD HALL
HOTEL AND BUSINESS CENTRE

### SWEET PASTRY

Roll out pastry to approximately 3mm being careful not to tear it. Grease tart case with Trenwax.

Line with greaseproof paper and then line case with pastry still being careful not to tear - ensuring the pastry is pushed to the corners of the case, rest in the fridge and then trim off any excess pastry.

Fill pastry case with baking rice and bake in the oven at 150°C for 15-20 minutes.

Meanwhile, on a low heat, place the sugar and butter in a thick bottomed pan and emulsify the sugar and butter together until the sugar has melted.

Crack the eggs into a bowl and whisk until blended together - add sugar mix and flour slowly still whisking so that the eggs do not scramble.

Pour into tart case previously filled with pecan nuts then bake at 140°C until set.

160g organic brown sugar

160g organic butter

2 eggs

15g organic flour

pinch of salt

200g pecan nuts

### SWEET PASTE

Cream the butter and sugar, add eggs then sieved flour. Cover in cling film and refrigerate overnight.

125g sugar

125g butter

1 egg

15g ground almonds (optional)

150g flour

# WE WOULD LIKE TO THANK THE FOLLOWING FOR THEIR SUPPORT:

Electrical and Mechanical Services

RAF Marham

The Haberdashers' Company

 **W. Vinten Limited**

CONCORDE CONSULTANTS LIMITED

INDEPENDENT FINANCIAL ADVISERS

RAF Brüggen

Congham Hall, Congham, Norfolk

Fishes' Restaurant, Burnham Market, Norfolk

Lynford Hall, Nr Thetford, Norfolk

Morston Hall, Morston, Norfolk

Rococos, King's Lynn, Norfolk

The Lifeboat Inn, Thornham, Norfolk

# CONVERSION TABLE

## Weights

| oz | g |
|---|---|
| 1/2oz | 10g |
| 3/4 | 20 |
| 1 | 25 |
| 1 1/2 | 40 |
| 2 | 50 |
| 2 1/2 | 60 |
| 3 | 75 |
| 4 | 110 |
| 4 1/2 | 125 |
| 5 | 150 |
| 6 | 175 |
| 7 | 200 |
| 8 | 225 |
| 9 | 250 |
| 10 | 275 |
| 12 | 350 |
| 1lb | 450 |
| 1lb 8oz | 700 |
| 2 | 900 |
| 3 | 1.35kg |

## Dimensions

| inch | |
|---|---|
| 1/8 inch | 3mm |
| 1/4 | 5mm |
| 1/2 | 1cm |
| 3/4 | 2 |
| 1 | 2.5 |
| 1 1/4 | 3 |
| 1 1/2 | 4 |
| 1 3/4 | 4.5 |
| 2 | 5 |
| 2 1/2 | 6 |
| 3 | 7.5 |
| 3 1/2 | 9 |
| 4 | 10 |
| 5 | 13 |
| 5 1/4 | 13.5 |
| 6 | 15 |
| 6 1/2 | 16 |
| 7 | 18 |
| 7 1/2 | 19 |
| 8 | 20 |
| 9 | 23 |
| 9 1/2 | 24 |
| 10 | 25.5 |
| 11 | 28 |
| 12 | 30 |

## Volume

| | |
|---|---|
| 2fl oz | 55ml |
| 3 | 75 |
| 5 (1/4 pt) | 150 |
| 10 (1/2 pt) | 275 |
| 1 pt | 570 |
| 1 1/4 | 725 |
| 1 3/4 | 1 litre |
| 2 | 1.2 |
| 2 1/2 | 1.5 |
| 4 | 2.25 |

## Oven temperatures

| Gas mark | °F | °C |
|---|---|---|
| 1 | 275 | 140 |
| 2 | 300 | 150 |
| 3 | 325 | 170 |
| 4 | 350 | 180 |
| 5 | 375 | 190 |
| 6 | 400 | 200 |
| 7 | 425 | 220 |
| 8 | 450 | 230 |
| 9 | 475 | 240 |

## USING THE RECIPES

1. As conversions from metric to imperial cannot always be exact, please follow either metric or imperial measurements throughout the recipe.

2. We advise that all meat, poultry, fish and eggs should be cooked thoroughly.

3. Some of the recipes include nuts or nut derivatives. These should not be eaten by pregnant or breast feeding women, children or those with nut allergies.

4. Recipes that contain soft ripened cheeses or continental products should not be eaten by children, the elderly, or pregnant or breast feeding women.

RECIPES FROM THE FRONT LINE

# INDEX

Copies of *Recipes From The Front Line*
can be ordered by contacting the
Royal Air Force Benevolent Fund Enterprises:
By telephone: 01285 713456
By post: Royal Air Force Benevolent Fund Enterprises
Dept. MAR 000
PO Box 1940
Fairford
Gloucestershire
GL7 4NA